REASSESSING AND RESTRUCTURING PUBLIC AGENCIES

Elizabeth Wiley MA JD

Elder, Pomo Nation, California USA

Order this book online at www.trafford.com
or email orders@trafford.com

Most Trafford titles are also available at major online book retailers.

Print information available on the last page.

ISBN: 978-1-4907-8445-8 (sc)
ISBN: 978-1-4907-8447-2 (hc)
ISBN: 978-1-4907-8446-5 (e)

Library of Congress Control Number: 2017913578

Because of the dynamic nature of the Internet, any web addresses or links contained in
this book may have changed since publication and may no longer be valid. The views
expressed in this work are solely those of the author and do not necessarily reflect the
views of the publisher, and the publisher hereby disclaims any responsibility for them.

Any people depicted in stock imagery provided by Thinkstock are models,
and such images are being used for illustrative purposes only.
Certain stock imagery © Thinkstock.

Trafford rev. 09/16/2017

 www.trafford.com
North America & international
toll-free: 1 888 232 4444 (USA & Canada)
fax: 812 355 4082

BEFORE:

I was raised to lead a nation. Our Nation was a Matriarchal Nation, one run by the Elder women, we called the Aunts. The reason for this was the systematic genocide of the Native California people, the men and older boys stayed behind, murdered, or caught and sold as slaves, to allow the women, children and old men to escape to the mountains and be saved. My Father was from this Nation. My Mother was rich, white and educated. A woman who led many of our Native American people, especially the women to get an education, to pursue their dreams and learn how to succeed in a world alien to our culture, while respecting the culture of our own Native Nation at the same time.

In one day, due to the parents divorce I joined the back and forth marathon of divorced children. In one day's drive back or forth, I went from playing in the creek on the reservation, living in the silver trailer by the creek, to my second home, a mansion belonging to my Mother's Great –Aunt (by respect, not blood) who was a professor from Cal Tech and Cornell. With her half brother, and two sisters they traveled the world, gathered plant samples and catalogued and named plants and algae from all over the lands, waters and seas. They all taught botany in colleges and universities as well. We had a stable in the back where they used to keep their donkeys to carry scientific materials and food while on their exploration trips. They also had a real science lab in the back of the property, and plants they had brought back from all over the world to study. We had a pond with plants, animals and water growth from all over the world that they had studied.

I was the first reservation woman in our State to complete law school and was hired as the National Director of Juvenile and Family Justice for Indian Centers. My goal was to address the comprehensive issues of families and children and to create support programs for single mothers and their children on reservations and in urban centers to facilitate the bi-culturation necessary for being at peace with the dominant money culture and the family culture of Native Americans. I have a Masters in Bicultural Development Specialty, a very rare degree that addresses the respect of home culture and ability in the dominant money culture. I have all but the final signatures and defense of a paper (I wrote five) to a PhD in Organizational Management/Doctorate of Management for my graduate level research and work on "Reassessing and Restructuring Public Agencies". I had started with Public Administration, but being bedridden by what turned out to be cancer, I went to online, which had only business doctoral degree courses..

Twenty five years before, after passing the first part of the California State Bar in 20 minutes, it is a three hour examination, I got a sample in the mail of a product from a baby soap and oatmeal company. I spent eight years learning how to walk and talk well enough to hold hot horses for my younger son who was learning to be a horse trainer in performance barns and the track. It took a lot longer to start a racial tension and gang abatement project for which I was offered a fellowship and research program to do a real program in my research area. That is a whole other book (The name of the book is going to be "Big Liz, the Leader of the Gang, based on a newspaper article one of my sisters sent me of that title, the article was NOT about me, but we always loved the headline and I had it on my desktop in a frame). I received my MA and decided to stay in the field rather than to pursue a job in a university, or corporations as a specialist diversity chair or Director..

I was told the online school had ADA for a brain injured person. They did not. I did not have $16,000 to pay an editor for the APA grammar, so never received my PhD.

In the meantime our Native Nation had managed to get over what we call "the land steal deals" in which many reservations were just shut down, at gun point, with military busses and bulldozers. The animals simply shot and killed by snipers as the busses pulled away and the bulldozers moved in on hundreds of years of survival, and thousands of years of culture. The people deposited in projects around the country where no one wanted them. The other minorities had no idea who they were, or why they were dumped in their projects, and the whites who did not want the minorities they had, let alone another bunch. After one Chair who was supported and put on us by a lawyer we finally got rid of with a BIA audit that showed she was not a legal member of our nation, we Elders talked and decided we should add respect to our Native men and supported one of my cousins for Chair. It has been a hard, and often thankless job, I hope he knows at least some of us really are grateful for his work, and sacrifices on our behalf.

I had gone to study for my PhD for two reasons: One to get paid for the programs and grants I kept inventing and getting grants for, only to be told they would be hiring a PhD to run my program; two, to give myself the discipline to see what could be done to change the runaway bureaucracy that was ruining America. I knew there had to be an answer, and after four years of research found it. THE MANUAL OF THE UNITED STATES GOVERNMENT. In this work I intended just to present my five papers. Over the time of writing it, the work has rewritten itself with the already in place ideas, visions and legislation that are more than adequate to facilitate a United States, and world that are free, and equal. The work of Eleanor Roosevelt and the vision for the United Nations are included in this book, "The Ten Rights and Responsibilities of the United Nations" is included in the form of a workbook we used for teaching the Codes of the United Nations to school children in the UN/USA programs across the world. We use these same codes and ideas to teach young people around the world the concepts of a world that functions with the stated principles of the Constitution, that ALL people have a RIGHT to life, liberty and the pursuit of happiness.

REASSESSING AND RESTRUCTURING PUBLIC AGENCIES

A Research Project of Spirit Horse II

Spirit Horse II
Animal Animal Assisted Therapy

Elizabeth Wiley, MA, JD Trainer/Director

Introduction:

Working with others, and in big projects, one begins to see a pattern of waste and silliness. This thought came to me, and I began to look for an answer. Why did we need multi-million dollar surveys to tell us how many homeless vets there were? Wouldn't it make better sense to spend the money putting vets in housing? How come we don't ask questions such as WHY are the vets homeless and answer in a positive way? BY creating housing that included treatment programs and new projects developed with the help of the veterans themselves to serve themselves and other veterans better!

In the segment on the Veteran's Administration, we did a simple thing. We drove around and saw how many people with signs noting they were homeless vets and needing help. Just driving around, we saw that even if one in ten were telling the truth, veterans were not getting taken care of. They were begging on street corners.

Then we began to stop and talk to those with signs. They told us that they were not allowed to have pets, they were treated worse than convicts in jail, and they had ALL their money taken away and given only $35 cash back for the month from the Board and Cares found by the VA for them to live in. One young vet with cancer was thrown out of the process for help because he honestly told the caseworker that he stood on a corner and gathered ten dollars a day to be allowed to sleep on the floor of a friend's house. WHAT?!?

Some of them were paying more than $1000 a month to live in a room with two other persons, and eat food the owners of the Board and Care were getting from food banks. That was not OK. No wonder they were out on the corner begging money for clothes, snacks, real food, any type of entertainment. Then I began to look around at others "serviced" in public agencies. It was an appalling look-see. The workers were the harshest critics of the programs. Many of the Administrators felt hog tied and not able to do anything to help those they had hired on to help.

While researching how to get help for some clients I came across in my volunteer work, I talked to a high administrator of a government agency who made a surprising statement: "If you ever get a clue, let me know, I don't have one".

At first I thought, then why did you take the job.

After the research for my PaPHooeyDegree, I found out what he meant. I had spoken to the Directors and high administrators of many Federal, County and Local agencies. They all seemed to be stymied by regulations that further research showed were put in place by lobbyist endeavors for the people that would be best served by those agencies not functioning properly.

I knew there had to be an answer. Our system does not leave us without one. Benjamin Franklin, Thomas Jefferson and others warned us to be eternally vigilant or we would lose our freedoms. Public scrutiny, transparency in government, freedom of the press are all oversight guarantors to make sure our agencies are doing the best job of their duty, for the best, most efficient cost. At the time of Franklin, the government had to raise money, and taxed only specifics, there was no income tax. Estate tax was developed to stop monopolies by families as had happened in so many other countries. The Boston Tea Party was a protest of settlers against the taxes being levied upon them by the Crown. The country America, long before it was a country had begun to resist anyone taxing the People and using the money against the will of the People. The Founders were intense in their desire to create a government that would not be able to be taken over by the few greedy, self aggrandizing persons wanting to have control of everything and everyone. I was told the Constitution and the work of the Founders of America was not a proper research support for a research study concerning government agencies. I disagree. Those premises are the only valid criteria for a study of reassessing and restructuring government agencies to meet their enabling legislation goals, set by the Congresses that had established the agencies.

As I delved into my research, I began to see that the vigilance had fallen well behind. Many realities, such as Kent State, and the Los Angeles Plaza Hotel, and riots as well as the deaths of many people who had been saying "be vigilant" did seem to be a damper on being vigilant, it seemed that it was time for the People to step up and get their freedoms back. The media is not free, it spoon feeds the public what the people most likely to benefit from the public NOT knowing do NOT need to hear, and prevents the publication of the truth if it threatens the bottom line to the media advertisers. That surely is not the Constitutional goal of free press. The current arguments regarding "fake" news seem to support a theory on both sides that the media reports not news, but a strange form of what the advertisers approve of, and what will get people to watch the shows to see the advertising. That would be two or three other dissertations, so will not be further discussed.

Each of the chapters in this book was once an attempt at a Dissertation. I was very specific when I came to the school that I wanted a certain topic, and had to do a certain dissertation to further my career as I had no other reason for getting a PaPhooey Degree than to create the paper necessary to get paid for my own projects after I got grants for them. I was very clear, I did not want to create any more programs, get grants for them and then be told someone else with a PhD was going to get the money and the program Director position because I did not have a PhD.

I also was very clear that the subject had to be "Reassessing and Restructuring Public Agencies". I was not able to get through the bias of the mentors who felt grammar was more important than content, even though I had been assured before I even registered by the DEAN that my ADA brain injuries which would make it impossible for me to do the grammar without an editor, paid for by my loans would come into their programs and not to worry, just think out of the box. I had worked at Cal Tech and gotten the assurance and promise of a

Department Chair who LOVED and taught statistics that he personally would help me when the time came to not just set up the research to code properly, but to help me learn how to read and utilize the material and put it into my paper.

I am very peeved about the outcome. I got 3.74 on my overall grades, including statistics which I had to take over, WITHOUT the promised editor, but did pass, even with my brain injuries. I wrote FIVE papers and did the research for FIVE papers. I did not get a mentor that was ADA brain injury certified, or the promised editor which UCLA and other schools assured me, when I did research to see what their policies were, would have happened at their schools.

I was told that the big schools ALL had the policy with brain injuries to take the recommendations of the student's own neurologist. MY neurologist, on my ADA requests when I started the admission process said that I would need help with the reading, writing and editing, and that I had such great talent and experience it was well worth working with me to do the parts of grammar and statistics to get my degree so I could get PAID for the work I had been doing for decades since I was disabled.

The school said OH YES, but in the end, demanded $16,000 for an editor they would not get me student loans to cover,and left me with over $73,000 of student loan debt, as well as more than $30,000 I had borrowed from family and friends and repaid, and use of my own money over several years to accomplish my goal.

There is no excuse for any of this.

When I contacted several large universities they told me that in their programs brain injured students were given special support as requested or suggested by their own neurologists. My doctor wrote that I should have the editors I needed since the work I was doing was so important and so successful, and I was providing much of it for free as well as training others to utilize the programs for free. He also wrote that just because I was not able to do the APA I should not be precluded from a PhD for which I had the experience, and skills to accomplish. They gave much less disabled people expensive special computers, and money for chairs, etc while even another student, a veteran was not given the mentor and editor to get the final paper signed off. Some years later, as I attempted once again to rebuild my goals after surviving cancer, one school did tell me that they just plain were not going to work with ADA brain injured students. I think that is a horrible discrimination, especially in face of the fact that this war is returning the largest number of brain injured veterans of any war ever, and car accidents are providing many other citizens with brain injuries that limit their ability to fit in to an increasingly nit picking paperwork system if a person wants to work. Currently it appears form complaints that even sports are churning out large numbers of brain injured disabled persons, who need rights within their abilities, not to just be shut out.

I had level four, stage four uterine and endometrial cancer diagnosed in my first year of graduate school. I still completed and did all my program. During my research I talked and emailed with experts and professors in the field of reassessing and restructuring public agencies. There are many wonderful people with amazing ideas of how to make our government run better, with better oversight, for less money. My work then became to document the research and to select a research area that would prove up one point in the career I had set for myself, to make sure that we have a system that works, for less money, that operates within the enabling legislations of the Title programs that initiated the agencies.

I would like to mention here that TITLE programs are seriously considered programs that THE PEOPLE agreed to when they worked WITH their Congresspersons. Often, programs such as TITLE programs for Native Nations persons, NOT just Native Americans, who are given special benefits in their treaties WITH the United States, even though mostly FORCED in illegal behavior in undeclared wars, those benefits can NOT be removed just because some decades down the road stingy persons without the knowledge of HOW our country works want those lands, assets and money used in the TITLE programs.

The five agencies I chose (or were thrust upon me by mentors) were:

• The Veteran's Administration, which included serious research into the Department of Defense and the promises made to those recruited and the breach of promise in those promises and contracts as they applied to the Veteran's Administration.

• The Bureau of Indian Affairs (which is part of the Bureau of Land Management for the Department of the Interior)

• FEMA, this was suggested by a mentor, how did people feel FEMA had done from one fire/flood year to the next crisis a year later. FEMA was changed in to a subsidiary department of Homeland Security while I was working on this research.

• The Department of Health and Human Services, HUD and housing. The research included the Title programs that began with the Roosevelt legislation that made it clear the PEOPLE of the United States were not going to allow small groups of people to use law, and force to take over everything and leave others with nothing on our American lands, and territories. The President of the United States was given the duty that could NOT be shirked, that NO person should suffer the effects of poverty, these were one by one outlined in the Manual of The United States Government, but were removed illegally by another administration decades later. The Manual of the United States Government states clearly that NOTHING can be changed in those laws and legislations without PUBLIC knowledge and hearings and full Congress votes......That has been just stepped over. This too would be another area of several dissertation level research projects to find the facts, and create a research project with an end goal of giving it to the United States Senate, Department of Justice and President at the time of the research being completed for investigation of the laws of our country being simply ignored or set aside for benefit of special interests.

- The Department of Education WITH The Department of Health and Human Services as it pertains to children and families, this included The Department of Justice as it pertains to children and families. I narrowed the study itself to Health and Human Services, certification and oversight of programs (I chose as a specific study Equine Therapy as it is another of my career choices to focus upon)

Each of the papers was properly formatted, for the purposes of this book, only the first one is presented as a Dissertation. The other four exclude much of the introductory material already covered during the discussions of the Veteran's Administration.

Much of the research showed excessive and vague overlapping of agencies for much of the work that must be done. This has created large amounts of paperwork, duplicity and the bureaucratic marshland that forced me to see the reasoning behind the statement noted above by one of the administrators I contacted. It was often almost impossible to figure out who was on first, and who was on second, let alone who was the pitcher, or the batter. The referee, nowhere to be found. Often no one appeared to have an answer to HOW to get things necessary to American citizens, and legislated to be performed with and for American citizens completed. The answer: form another quasi agency or committee and create even more expense and confusion to the persons needing services and more cost to the taxpayers.

There is no excuse for any of this.

Benjamin Franklin said often that when government got too burdensome, it was time to rid ourselves of it, and start over with the Constitution and vision of our principles fully in mind and heart. I was wary enough not to put this type of statement in the Dissertations, I did not want to create an idea that I was anti-Government or some kind of revolutionary. I wanted to find an answer to the dilemma of spending too much money on programs that were not properly oversight managed for waste, and / or performance of the actual legislative intent for the agency.

This book explores the problems of agencies that exist today. It explores the legislative enabling intent of the Congress that created each agency. The United States Government Manual from 2004 is the base research guide for the stated reason the agency exists and taxpayer funds are allocated to fund that agency. Much of the material is paraphrased from The Manual of The United States Government itself, the author strongly suggests that taxpayers buy one, and then buy an old one, from 1950 or so, and compare them. IF we do not want to be just wage slaves, or worse yet, serfs in our own country, we NEED to KNOW what is going on and what our principles are and how to stand up for them.

The research project for each agency was a simple one. The goal was to create oversight that would at the same time inexpensively illustrate how the agency was doing the duty it was charged with by that enabling legislation (or sadly, NOT doing the duty it was charged to do by the Congress and People that founded the agency). Each agency is listed below for the project it contained:

- The Veterans Administration is charged with providing benefits to veterans. The oversight suggested project, which is related to the survey completed by veterans is simple: Are veterans being provided benefits? The paper is simple because it is for one simple goal, to get the dissertation process completed, therefore many larger aspects of each possible real survey are not addressed. The footnote to the chapter is about the Department of Defense. Do they owe more honesty to recruits about active duty, and about veterans problems they will face when they are injured or discharged?

- The Bureau of Indian Affairs. There are many facets of the BIA and what it is legislated to accomplish. The first page of the discussion details the burden of duty enacted by the enabling legislation. The survey process was to ask Native Americans how they feel the BIA is doing in meeting that duty. The comparison of the BIA's own performance reviews based on paperwork, rather than service and oversight was developed to show the need for straight forward performance review. The 2012 Abramoff hearings and investigations are added to this book to illustrate the insight his own confession and apology shed on the horrors inflicted on Native Americans by their own lawyers and lobbyists paid with Native American funds to work AGAINST their best interests as late as the 2000 casino debacles. Note: for those not up to reading a government hearing and investigation, just see the movie "Casino Jack" that Abramoff wrote while in prison for his actions in those events. The support documentation for his movie was the material he supplied to get a plea agreement and is available in many of the magazine and news articles and books written about the subject of his arrest.

- FEMA and the Department of Homeland Security. The question was, as suggested by a mentor, did FEMA improve its services from one fire/flood period in my local area to the same critical fire/flood period in the current year. I did not see this for any relevance to my original study, but have included the discussion of the research in this work.

- Health and Human Services. Housing is a very broad issue, The Agency needs to have interaction with many other agencies, such as banking, insurance, and State and local governments. The survey portion was kept simple, The question was, how is the agency meeting its legislated duty, look around and see homeless persons, the duty is not being met.

- The Department of Education, The Department of Health and Human Services and The Department of Justice in relation to the enabling legislation duties to provide children education, healthcare, safety, and justice. The survey was to talk to homeless, truant and abandoned youth and children. Just a few questions each. The goal was to show, as long as there are children homeless, truant and abandoned, the Departments are not meeting their duty.

Health and Human Services has the duty to certify health programs for payment by insurance companies and hospitals or clinics. Equine therapy was the subject I chose, as it has been more than forty years that the therapy programs have been asking for certification to get paid. The paper discusses the realities for the programs and how they are working out the problems of not getting paid directly for services that are expensive. The paper also discusses the research showing the success rates of this type of therapy at a cost much lower in human suffering, and to the taxpayers for long term lock down treatment of many persons that have successfully completed the programs. Note: currently equine therapy programs are getting paid under the umbrella of licensed therapists who are using the horses as outdoor couches, which is NOT equine therapy, it is psychotherapy on a horse.

The conclusion of much of this research is: The agencies put in place to help the citizens who pay for them have become a bureaucratic mess that no one, least of all their Administrators, knows how to deal with. For the pathetic taxpayer, it has become a tax nightmare and they require more and more money, to do less and less except to hire lawyers to make codes to exclude more and more of the taxpayers for the services they paid for! This statement is based on the information contained in boxes of paperwork from the Public Safety Officers Benefits appeals of the disabled mother of a Deputy shot by a gang member. This woman, over thirteen years of appeals, was constantly kept from her benefits by NEW regulations that changed the qualifying regulations and excluded her claim, even though the PSOB's own appeal officer initially found her to be eligible. The agency filed its appeal, fired its own appeal officer, and rewrote the regulations to exclude the premises upon which he had founded his judgment. She found many of the 9/11 first responders and their families going through the same harassment and nightmare. She also found an article that two of the lawyers hired to do this harassment had been indicted for deterring public funds from proper sources to vague ones in other agencies where it was NOT approved to be spent. Why would they then be hired to "help" the first responders beneficiaries by making more regulations to keep them from benefits. It makes no sense. While this information is document supported hearsay and not able to be used for a research project it is supported in the movie by Michael Moore regarding the 9/11 First Responders not being given care, so he took them to Cuba, which gave them FREE care and if you see the movie, it shows CARE, not bureaucracy.

Except for the lawyer for PSOB I spoke to in this matter, I did not find ONE SINGLE government employee or administrator who did not feel the money could be better spent to HELP those who needed help rather than exclude as many as possible who actually were eligible. I also did not find ONE SINGLE word of rationale for hiring up to 10,000 lawyers for the department of defense as revealed in the CSPAN covered Congressional investigation of the torture authorized by the Bush administration against all civilized codes of conduct for interrogation of prisoners of war. There is no excuse for hiring lawyers to find ways to NOT serve the taxpayers who pay for the services or benefits for those who serve the public, such as first responders and veterans instead of paying for benefits.

There are discussions contained in the chapters regarding benefits NOT being cash. There are also discussions and questions in surveys regarding the fact that people would rather get help and move on than be crippled by systems that belittle them and provide only enough to stay alive, and be demeaned. Somewhere the reality that the money for ALL of these programs comes from the taxpayers, and that the legislation was enabled to SERVE the taxpayers, and that there is not one single mission statement, enabling legislation or place in the Constitution that I could find that says "waste the taxpayers money, treat the taxpayers like beggars who are pestering you, and make sure to torment the ill, disabled, veterans, seniors and children at the taxpayers expense".

The first three chapters are taken from proposed dissertations, the next chapter is an overview of the agencies of the United States Government, as detailed annually in the published Manual of the United States Government. Every viable agency is required to have a statement and description of the Agency available by the due date for the manual to be assembled and published in a timely manner. The final chapters relate the material contained to the reality of oversight and reassessing and restructuring public agencies. The Constitution and the United Nations Ten Rights and Responsibilities of every human on earth are contained in the final chapters with discussion as to laws of the land, ethics, and morals. Recent cases have put forth the need for an international agreement on the handling of freedom of the press, and freedom of speech, as well as the necessity for any agency with the possibility to hide ethics violations and actions that can and may be construed as war crimes to have strict policy that is adhered to or the press can and will be notified through the process. This is discussed at length in those later chapters.

THE CONSTITUTION OF THE UNITED STATES OF AMERICA

(Both the Declaration and Constitution are shortened and discussed briefly)
It is strongly suggested that every resident of the United States read and understand the real documents. They are available online and in most college and university bookstores.

DECLARATION OF INDEPENDENCE

The Declaration of Independence started us on an adventure, a vision of a few men, many who had studied centuries of people's visions, plans and governments, to find out what they might think of to make a country that would last, that could fail, and rise up out of the ashes........these people did not all agree.

There were things they wrote that have over the years been explored by Americans and changed. We have figured out it was not the best policy to just take the land from the people who lived here, yet it has taken two hundred years and there still are problems along this line, as the two cultures clashed, not including the two to three hundred years of genocide preceding the founding of the United States and Constitution.

The Founders knew these changes would occur, appeared to have welcomed them, but gave us the power, through the Constitution and Declaration of Independence to pull back, look at our failures and restructure. In a book on reassessing and restructuring public agencies I felt the start needed to be the Declaration of Independence and Constitution. Not in their whole. Each American, whether legal or not, needs to read these documents and know what they are, take them to heart, and remind themselves that if we expect rights, we acquire responsibilities along with them.

To restructure an agency, one must look at what was supposed to be, what is, and what can be, and restructure to provide more of what the agency was designed for, rather than what the agency has become. In every example it becomes obvious that oversight needs to be a part of every part of an agency, to ensure the duty is being met, and that the taxpayers are not being defrauded by corruption in each agency.

The Declaration of Independence says that when a government becomes destructive of the rights declared in the Declaration of Independence and Constitution, PEOPLE have the RIGHT to alter or abolish that government.

Teaching high level Kindergarten, for very wealthy children, who will all have to test into the most exclusive private schools in the nation and world in January of the kindergarten year, at age 5, the children were taught the Declaration of Independence, the Constitution, the three areas of government, along with the solar system, the earth, and continents and ALL the states and territories of the United States of America. I think any person living in America deserves the same education, as well as has the responsibility to learn the responsibilities that go along with the rights and responsibilities of the Declaration of Independence, Constitution and Bill of Rights. In the end of this book I have put a copy of the book we use for the Ten Rights and Responsibilities work book for children and adults of all ages to learn and understand the concepts of the United Nations. We have a similar set of workbooks for the Constitution and Bill of Rights, and Declaration of Independence, which is in shortened form in this chapter.

DECLARATION OF INDEPENDENCE is one of three documents that are vital to every person in America to know, from their rights, to their responsibilities. These workbook pages are simple and plainly stated, easily translated to any other language for use by any person living in America who does not speak an American English.

In Congress: July 4 1776, the Congress and President of the United States of America finalized this document to formally establish The United States of America.

Inalienable Rights.

Life.

Liberty.

Pursuit of Happiness.

Equality.

Governments derive their just power from the governed.

When ANY form of Government becomes destructive of these ends..........

RIGHT of the People to alter or abolish it.

There are many complaints and allegations contained within the Declaration of Independence that as one reads them may pertain to today.

While the Declaration is speaking of the british king, the congress and other political, elected and appointed persons currently can be argued to at least have done this:

Erected multitudes of new offices, and sent hither swarms of Officers to harass our people, and eat out of their substance

Effected to render the Military independent of and superior to the Civil power

Deprived us, in many cases, the benefit of trial by jury

Plundered our seas, ravaged our coasts, (burnt) our towns, and destroyed the lives of our people It can be argued that taking of property or water, or other assets by a large town, county or another state without the CONSENT of those who own those rights in their own individual, city, county or state or country rights are plundering. It can be argued that forcing taxpayers to pay for wars that are to support empire building or protection of monarchs from other countries are plundering. It can be argued that pollution of water, air, and soil are ALL plundering that need to be addressed by our citizen's as Constitutional Rights.

These few statements apply to today, except lobbyists, and politicians have done these things, not a foreign power. The towns may not have burnt, but hurricanes, forest fires, foreclosures, no jobs, no water from fracking, no farms from lawsuits by patent lawyers over pollen that has wafted on the wind, or seeds that have fallen off trucks, have closed down our towns and left people as homeless and destitute as if the towns have been burnt.

The Declaration goes on to state that we, as United States, MUST stand up to change these acts against the citizens of The United States of America.

THE CONSTITUTION OF THE UNITED STATES OF AMERICA

Every person, citizen, visitor, foreign resident, child, adult needs to read the words and take them to heart to "secure the Blessings of Liberty" contained within the Constitution of the United States of America.

Even as the Constitution was written, the Native Americans, women, slaves, were not given the rights, but over the decades America has rectified at least some of these omissions.

The Preamble to the Constitution makes it clear with the word "posterity" that this document is meant to establish an ongoing government. Through wars, expansion, genocide of the original people of America, slavery, women being held as second class citizens, gays and others being allowed to be bullied and even tortured and killed, the Constitution has stood a test of time as The United States has struggled with problems and growth. The major depression of the early twentieth century gave birth to restrictions on the greedy and corruption, but those laws have been eroded by corruption. The Constitution gives us a place to look to in order to find our center, our balance and begin again.

The few words of the Constitution (52, without a period) are not APA approved, yet give the human race a vision and solid foundation to build a government OF the People, BY the People and FOR the People, if the People heed the warnings of the Founders and have constant vigil over the country. The Articles and Amendments add clarity and afterthoughts.

ARTICLE I. Section 1: ALL legislative powers shall be vested in Congress. This section needs to be read and understood by every voter. Congresspersons work for the People and create legislation. This article of the Constitution has taken a beating in the last sixty years as executive orders were added to agencies that have reduced the power not only of the People, but of Congress. CONGRESS can create legislation, but they have to get elected and NOT get recalled to be able to legislate. The PEOPLE are supposed to keep the POWER.

Section 2 tells how the House members can be elected. The Constitution says clearly that to be elected, the Representatives MUST be inhabitants of the State where they are to represent the people. At that time, those who wrote the Constitution argued, you can read their diaries, and newspaper and books regarding those arguments, but in the final argument, in order to get the Constitution signed, slaves, Native Americans, and debt bonded persons were not given the same ratio of a human right as a "free" man. Women were considered as free persons, but could not vote. The House of Representatives is given the sole authority to impeach. Today it is VERY important for the VOTERS of a district to make sure their Congressperson IS a RESIDENT, not just a rent payer on a walk up of their district. It is up to the VOTERS to say NO to outsiders who are just using an open seat to get into a career political job. THAT is NOT the intention of the Founders of our Nation. The intention was that a Representative LIVE in the area represented, to KNOW the voters and the issues and represent THE VOTERS, not outsiders.

Section 3 deals with the Senate and how they are appointed by the legislature of the state they come from. Today, Senators are elected by the People. Again, Senators must be inhabitants of the State they represent. The Vice President of the United States is the President of the Senate, but has no vote unless there is a tie. The Senate chooses their own officers and a Pro Tem President should the Vice President be absent, or have taken the office of President.

While the House is the sole authority to impeach, the Senate has the sole authority for trial for impeachment. The Chief Justice shall preside at impeachments of the President of The United States of America, and each member of the Senate takes an affirmation and oath prior to the impeachment commencing. A Senate must have a two thirds of the membership concur to impeach. While an impeachment has a loss of office, the person cannot hold another office of honor, the person is also still liable under indictment, trial, judgment and punishment by law as well.

Section 4 The time, place and manner of elections for each State for Senator and House Representatives is prescribed by the State in which the Congresspersons are elected. The Congress shall meet at least ONCE in each year, the date set was the first Monday of December, unless Congress changes the date.

Section 5. Each House shall be the Judge of Elections, Returns and Qualifications of its own Membership. A quorum is a majority of the House or Senate, but for day to day the House may set its own standard, and/or compel members to attend a meeting or vote, setting their own penalties for those who do not attend a mandatory vote or meeting. Each house creates its own rules of proceedings, punish members for disorderly behavior and with concurrence of two thirds of their members, expel a member.

Each House shall keep a journal of proceedings (these are kept in the archives and are accessible to the citizenry) except, as each House sees a certain portion secret. If one fifth of either House shall demand, a record of yay, or nay votes on an issues are to be published on the official journal.

Neither House, during the Session, shall, without the consent of the other House, adjourn for more than three days, nor to any other place than where the Houses are sitting. Note: they only met once a year in the first week of December.

Section 6: The Senators and Representatives shall receive a compensation for their services, to be ascertained by Law, The Members of both Houses, during the term of their election, be given immunity from arrest except for treason, felony or breach of the peace, during the session of their respective House, and in going to or returning from their House, and/or speeches and debates, nor questioned in any other place.

No member of either House is able to be appointed to any civil office under the authority of the United States, and no person in civil office may accept a seat in either House during continuance in office.

Section 7:

ALL bills for raising revenue shall originate in the House of Representatives, the Senate may propose or concur with Bills.

EVERY Bill, after passing the House and the Senate, shall be passed to the President for signature. The President can send a Bill back with objections as to refusal to sign. The originating House or Senate may consider changes, or send the Bill back with support, The House can Reconsider a Bill and pass it with a two thirds vote If the President fails to return a Bill within 10 days, Sundays are not included, the Bill is considered passed in to Law. An adjourned Congress can not force a Bill by being closed.

Section 8:

The Congress shall have power to lay and collect taxes, duties, imposts, and excises to pay the debts and provide for the common Defence and general welfare of the United States. This Section makes it mandatory that all taxes, duties, imposts and excises are uniform throughout the United States.

This Section give specific areas where Congress exercises power over the economy for the United States of America.

To borrow money on the credit of the United States

To regulate commerce with foreign nations, the several states, and Native American Nations.

To establish uniform Rules of Naturalization and Bankruptcies in any of the States

To coin money, regulate the value and the value of foreign coins, and fix the standards of weights and measures

To provide punishments for counterfeiting coin and Securities

To establish post offices and Post Roads

To promote the progress of Science and the useful arts by securing for limited times patents and copyrights to authors and inventors to respective writings and discoveries.

To constitute Tribunals inferior to the Supreme Court

To define and punish piracy and felonies upon the high seas and offences against the Laws of Nations

To declare War, grant letters of Marque and Reprisal and make rules about captures on land and water

To raise and support Armies, NO appropriation of Money to that use shall be for a term longer than TWO years

To provide and maintain a Navy

To make rules for government and regulation of land and naval forces.

To provide for calling forth the Militia to execute the Laws of the Unionn, to suppress insurrections and repel invasions

To provide the organization and arming of the militia, reserving to the States to appoint the officers of their State militia and the training of their State militia according to the disciplines set by Congress

To have exclusive Legislation in all cases over Washington DC, the seat of the Federal Government, as well as all Federal bases established by Congress in States.

To make all Laws necessary and proper to carry on the Executive foregoing powers, and all other Powers vesting by the Constitution in the Government of the United States, or any Department of Officer thereof.

Section9:

The immigration laws shall not be limited by Congress prior to 1808, and no tax on immigration shall exceed $10.

No Bill of Attainder or ex post facto Law can be passed.

The privilege of Writ of Habeas Corpus shall not be suspended unless a case of rebellion or invasion of the public safety may require it.

No capitation or other direct tax shall be laid unless in proportion to the census or enumeration herein before directed to be taken

No tax or duty will be laid on articles exported from any state.

No preference shall be given by any regulation or revenue to one port over another, nor shall vessels bound for one be forced enter, clear, or pay duties to another.

No money shall be drawn from the treasury, but in Consequence of Appropriations made by Law. A regular statement of Account of the Receipts and payments must be made public from time to time of ALL PUBLIC money.

No title of nobility shall be granted by the United States. No person holding ANY office of profit or trust, shall, without the consent of Congress accept any present, emolument, Office or Title of any kind whatsoever from any King, Prince or foreign State.

Section 10:

No state shall enter into any Treaty Alliance or confederation, grant letters of Marque and Reprisal, coin money, emit Bills of Credit, make any thing but gold or silver coin a tender to pay debts, pass any bill of Attainder or ex post facto law, or law impairing the obligation of contracts, or grant any title of nobility.

No state shall, without consent of Congress lay any imposts or duties on imports or exports, except what may be absolutely necessary for executing inspection laws, the net produce of all duties and imposts, laid by any State on Imports or exports shall be for use of the Treasury of the United States and all such laws shall be subject to revision and control by Congress.

No state shall without consent of Congress, lay any duty of tonnage, keep troops, ships of war in time of peace, enter into agreements or compacts with any state or foreign power, or engage in War, unless actually invaded or in such imminent danger as will not admit of delay.

ARTICLE II

The Executive Power of the President is clarified in Article II of the Constitution.

The large second section of Article II is the Electoral College, establishing how each State shall elect a President and Vice President. This is an interesting segment to read, as one sentence states that the Electors (a group established by each State legislature, to equal the same as their number of Senators and Representatives) should elect two persons, one of whom should not be an inhabitant of their own state. The person with the greatest number shall be President, the second greatest number of votes Vice President. The one elected must have at least a majority. If more than one has a majority, the Representatives will then vote at least two thirds of the Members for the President. If this results in equal votes, the Senate shall break the tie.

This has been changed as explained below in the Amendments to a certain degree, and parties were added.

The President must be at least 35 years old, a citizen from birth, and must have lived fourteen years within the United States.

If a President dies in office, or is removed, impeached, resigns, or is disabled the Vice President will take the office of President, until disability is removed or a new President is elected.

The President shall receive compensation which shall not be increased, or decreased during the period of office elected to serve, he shall not receive any other Emolument from the United States, or any State.

The Oath of office "I do solemnly swear (or affirm)that I will faithfully execute the office of President of the United States, and will to the best of my Ability, preserve, protect and defend the Constitution of the United States."

Section 2:

The President shall be Commander in Chief of the Army and Navy of the United States, and the militia of the States when called into Service OF the United States. He may require an Opinion, in writing of the Principal officer in each of the executive offices, and shall have the power to grant reprieves and pardons for offences against the Unite States, except in of impeachment.

He shall have Power, by and with the Advice and consent of the Senate to make Treaties, provided two thirds of the Senators present concur and shall nominate by and with the advice and consent of the Senate, appoint ambassadors, public ministers, consuls, judges of the Supreme Court and all other Officers of the United States are not herein otherwise provided for and which shall be established by Law, Congress may, by Law vest the Appointment of such inferior officers as they think proper, in the President alone, in the courts of law or in the heads of departments.

The President shall fill up vacancies that may happen during the recess of the Senate, by granting commissions which shall expire at the end of their next session.

Section 3:

He shall, from time to time give to Congress information from the State of the Union, and recommend to their consideration measures as he judges necessary and expedient, he may, on extraordinary occasion, convene both Houses or either of them, and in case of disagreement between them with respect to the time of adjournment, he may adjourn them to such a time he shall deem proper, he shall receive ambassadors and other public ministers, he shall take care that the Laws be faithfully executed and shall commission all the officers of the United States.

Section 4:

The President, Vice President and all civil officers of he Unite States shall be removed from office on impeachment for and conviction of, treason, bribery, or other high crimes and misdemeanors.

ARTICLE III

Section 1

The judicial power of the United States shall be vested in one Supreme Court and such inferior courts as Congress may from time to time ordain and establish. The judges shall hold their offices during good Behaviour and at stated time receive for their services, compensation that can not be diminished during their continuance in Office.

Section 2

The Judicial Power shall extend to all cases, in Law and Equity, arising under this Constitution,

the Laws of the United States,

and Treaties made or which shall be made under their authority,

to all cases involving ambassadors, other public ministers and consuls,

to all cases of admirality and maritime jurisdiction,

to controversies with the United States shall be a party,

to controversies between two or more states,

between citizens of another state, between citizens of different states,

between citizens of the same state claiming lands under grants of different states

and between a state or citizens thereof and foreign states, citizens or subjects.

In all cases affecting ambassadors, other public ministers and consuls and those in which a state shall be a party, the supreme court shall have original jurisdiction. All the other mentioned cases the supreme court shall have appellate jurisdiction, both as to Law and Fact, under such regulations as the Congress shall make.

The trial of all crimes, except in cases of impeachment, shall be by jury and held in the state where the crimes were committed, when not committed within any state, the trail shall be at a place Congress may by law have directed.

Section 3:

Treason against the United States shall consist only in levying War against the United States or in adhering to their enemies, giving them aid and comfort No person shall be convicted of Treason unless on the testimony of two witnesses of the same event or on confession in open court.

Congress shall have the power to declare the punishment of treason, but no attainder of treason shall work corruption of blood or forfeiture except during the life of the person attained.

ARTICLE IV

Section 1:

Full faith and credit shall be given in each state to the public acts, records, and judicial proceedings of every other state. And Congress may by general laws prescribe the manner in which such acts records, and proceedings be proved and the effect thereof.

Section 2:

The citizens of each sate shall be entitled to all privileges and immunities of the several states.

A person charged in any state with treason, felony or other crime who shall flee from justice, and be found in another state, shall on demand of the executive authority of the state from which he fled, be delivered up, to be removed to the state having jurisdiction over the crime.

No person held to service or labour in one state, under the laws thereof, escaping into another shall in consequence of any law or regulation therein, be escaping from service or labour, but shall be delivered up on claim of the party to whom such service or labour is due. (This is about slavery and indebted servitude-as the Amendments appear, this is addressed by Congress and changed).

Section 3:

New States may be admitted by Congress into this Union, but no new State shall be formed or erected within the jurisdiction of any other State, nor any State be formed by the junction of two or more states or parts of states, without the consent of the legislatures of the States concerned as well as Congress.

The Congress shall have Power to dispose of land and make all needful Rues and regulations respecting the territory or other property belonging to the United States. Nothing in this Constitution shall be so construed as to prejudice any claims of the United

States or of any particular State. (This is an important section, it leaves the actual land disputes to the courts and if appealed and accepted, to the Supreme Court itself, rather than to have wars, or insurrections between the states).

Section 4:

The United States shall guarantee to every State in this Union a Republican form of Government, and shall protect each of them against invasion, and on application of the legislature, or of the executive (when legislature can not be convened) against domestic violence.

ARTICLE V

The Congress, with two thirds of both Houses deeming it necessary, shall propose Amendments to this Constitution, or on application of the legislatures of two thirds of the several states, shall call a convention for proposing amendments which in either case shall be valid to all intents and purposes as part of this Constitution when ratified by three fourths of the several States or by conventions in three fourths thereof as one mode or the other may be proposed by Congress. Provided that no Amendment be made prior to 1808that shall affect the first and fourth clauses in the Ninth Section of the First Article, and that no state, without its consent shall be deprived of its equal suffrage in the Senate.

(This article is important in discussions later in this book, regarding changes either made, or needing to be made in the United States).

ARTICLE VI

All debts contracted and engagements entered into before the adoption of the Constitution, shall be valid against the United States under this Constitution, as under the confederation.

This Constitution and the laws of the United States which shall be made in pursuance thereof, and all treaties made, or which shall be made under the authority of the United States shall be the Supreme Law of the land and the Judges in every state shall be bound thereby any thing in the Constitution or laws of any state to the contrary notwithstanding.

The senators and Representatives mentioned before, and the Members of the several state legislatures and all executive and judicial officers, both of of the United States and of the several States shall be bound by oath or affirmation to support this Constitution, but no religious test shall ever be required as a qualification to any office or public trust under the United States.

ARTICLE VII

The ratification of the conventions of nine States shall be sufficient for the establishment of this Constitution between the states so ratifying the same. The signatures are included from the original ratifications.

The First Ten Amendments were known as the Bill of Rights

AMENDMENT I

Congress shall make NO law respecting the establishment of religion or prohibiting the free exercise thereof, or abridging the freedom of speech, or of the press, or of the right of the people peaceably to assemble and to petition the Government for a redress of grievances.

AMENDMENT 2

A well regulated militia being necessary to the security of a free state, the right of the people to keep and bear arms shall not be infringed.

AMENDMENT 3

No soldier shall, in time of peace, be quartered in any house, without the consent of the Owner, nor in time of war, but in a manner to be prescribed by law.

AMENDMENT 4

The right of the people to be secure in their persons, houses, papers, and effects against all unreasonable searches and seizures, shall not be violated and no warrants shall issue, but upon probably cause or affirmation and particularly describing the place to be searched or the persons or things to be seized.

AMENDMENT 5

No persona shall be held to answer for a capital or otherwise infamous crime, unless on a presentment or indictment of a grand jury, except in cases arising in the land or naval forces or in the militia when in actual service in time of war or public danger, nor shall any person be subject for the same offence to be twice put in the jeopardy of life or limb, nor shall be compelled in any criminal case to be a witness against himself, nor be deprived of life, liberty or property, without due process of law, nor shall private property be taken for public use without just compensation.

AMENDMENT 6

In all criminal prosecutions, the accused shall enjoy the right to a speedy and public trial, by an impartial jury of the State and district wherein the crime shall have been committed, which district shall have been previously ascertained by law, and to be informed of the nature and cause of the accusation, to be confronted with witnesses against him, to have compulsory process for obtaining witnesses in his favor, and to have the assistance of counsel for his defence.

AMENDMENT 7

In suits at common law, where the value in controversy shall exceed twenty dollars, the right of trial by jury shall be preserved, and no fact tried by a jury shall be otherwise re-examined in any Court of the United States, than according to the rules of common law.

AMENDMENT 8

Excessive bail shall not be required, or excessive fines imposed, nor cruel and unusual punishments inflicted

AMENDMENT 9

The enumeration in he Constitution of certain rights, shall not be construed to deny or disparage others retained by the people

AMENDMENT 10

The powers not delegated to the United States by the Constitution not prohibited by it to the states are reserved to the states respectively or to the people.

AMENDMENT 11

Ratified February 7, 1795

The judicial power of the United States shall not be construed to extend to any suit in law or equity, commenced or prosecuted against one of the United States by citizens of another state, or by citizens or subjects of any foreign stated

AMENDMENT 12

Ratified July 27, 1804

The Electors shall meet in their respective states and vote by ballot for President and Vice President, one of whom, at least, shall not be an inhabitant of the same state with themselves.

President and vice President shall be on separate votes (this is a change from the original most votes President, next Vice President) The rules in this Amendment are lengthy and no longer apply, but will be discussed as the Amendments change this Amendment.

No vice presidential candidate can be on the ballot unless qualified by the Constitutional regulations to be President should that need arise.

AMENDMENT 13

Ratified December 6, 1865

Section 1 Neither slavery nor involuntary servitude, except as punishment for crime wherein the party shall have been duly convicted, shall exist within the United States or any place subject to their jurisdiction

Section 2 Congress shall have power to enforce this article by appropriate legislation

(This is an important important Amendment, it negates the clauses in Article IV that in essence demand that any state return runaway slaves, or runaway indentured servants).

AMENDMENT 14

Ratified July 9, 1868

Section 1:

All persons born or naturalized in the United States and subject to the jurisdiction thereof, are citizens of the United States and of the States wherein they reside. NO STATE shall make or enforce any law which shall abridge or the privileges or immunities of citizens of the United States, nor shall any State deprive any person of life, liberty or property, without due process of law, nor deny to any person within its jurisdiction the equal protection of the law.

Section 2:

Representatives shall be apportioned among the several States according to their respective numbers, counting the whole number of the persons in each State, excluding

Indians (Native Americans) not taxed. Male citizens, over 21 are given the right to vote and to be given that same right in any state.

(This is another important, important Amendment, it shows the depth of racism, genderism and rules to keep the "people" from being part of the "people", as well as shows how far the country has expanded in rights over the next 150 years as new Amendments were hard fought, won and put in place).

Section 3:

No person shall be a Senator or Representative in Congress or elector of President or Vice President, or hold any office, civil or military, under the United States, or under any State who, having previously taken an oath, as a member of Congress or as an officer of the United States, or as a member of any State legislature, or as an executive or judicial officer of any State to support the Constitution of the United States, shall have engaged in insurrection or rebellion against the same, or given aid or comfort to the enemies thereof. But Congress may by a vote of two thirds of each House, remove such disability.

Section 4:

The validity of the public debt of the United States, authorized by law, including debts incurred for payment of pensions and bounties for services in suppressing insurrection or rebellion, shall not be questioned. But neither the United States nor any State shall assume or pay any debt or obligation incurred in aid of insurrection or rebellion against the United States, or any claim for the loss or emancipation of any slave; but all such debts, obligations, and claims shall be held illegal and void.

Section 5:

The Congress shall have the power to enforce by appropriate legislation, the provision of this article.

AMENDMENT 15

Ratified February 3, 1870

Section 1:

The right of citizens of the United States to vote shall not be denied or abridged by the United States or any State on account of race, color, or previous condition of servitude.

Section 2:

The Congress shall have power to enforce this article by appropriate legislation.

AMENDMENT 16

Ratified February 3, 1913

The Congress shall have power to lay and collect taxes on income, from whatever source derived, without apportionment among the several states and withut regard to any census or enumeration.

AMENDMENT 17

Ratified April 8, 1913

The Senate of the United States shall be composed of two Senators from each State, elected by the People thereof for six years, and each Senator shall have one vote. The electors in each State shall have the qualifications requisite for electors of the most numerous branch of the State legislatures.

When vacancies happen in the Representation of any State in the Senate, the executive authority of such state shall issue writs of election to fill such vacancies; PROVIDED, That the legislature of any State may empower the executive thereof to make temporary appointments until the people fill the vacancies by election as the legislature may direct.

This amendment shall not be so construed as to affect the term of any Senator chosen before it becomes valid as part of the Constitution.

AMENDMENT 18

Ratified January 16, 1919, repealed December 5, 1933.

This was the law against manufacture, sale, distribution and transport of intoxicating liquors within the United States.

AMENDMENT 19

The right of citizens of the United States to vote shall not be denied or abridged by the United States or by any State on account of sex.

Congress shall have the power to enforce this article by appropriate legislation.

AMENDMENT 20

Ratified January 23, 1933

Section 1:

The terms of President and Vice President shall end at noon on the 20th day of January, and the terms of Senators and Representatives at noon on the 3rd day of January, of the years in which such terms would have ended if this article had not been ratified, and the terms of their successors shall then begin.

Section 2:

The Congress shall assemble at least ONCE in every year, and such meeting shall begin at noon on the 3rd day of January, unless they shall by law appoint a different day.

Section 3:

If, at the time fixed for the beginning of a term of President, the President elect shall have died, the Vice President elect shall become President. If a President shall not have been chosen before the time fixed for the beginning of his term or if the President elect shall have failed to qualify, then the Vice President elect shall act as President until shall have qualified, and the Congress may by law provide for the case where neither a President elect nor a Vice President elect shall have qualified, declaring who shall then act as President, or in the manner in which one who is to act shall be selected, and such person shall act accordingly until a President or Vice President shall have qualified.

Section 4:

The Congress may by law provide for the case of the death of any of the persons from whom the House of Representatives may choose a President whenever the right of choice shall have devolved upon them, and for the case of the death of any of the persons from whom the Senate may choose a Vice President whenever the right of choice shall have devolved upon them.

Section 5

Sections 1 and 2 shall take effect on the 15th day of October following the ratification of this article

Section 6

This article shall be inoperative unless it shall have been ratified as an amendment to the Constitution by the legislatures of three fourths of the several states within seven years from the date of its submission.

AMENDMENT 21

Ratified December 5, 1933

Section 1

The eighteenth article is hereby repealed.

Intoxicating liquors become legal once again.

AMENDMENT 22

Ratified February 27, 1951

Section 1

No person shall be elected to the office of the President more than twice, and no person who has held the office of President or acted as President for more than two years of a term to which some other person was elected.

This Article does not apply to the person holding the office of President at the time of this ratification, nor does it prevent any person who is President more than two terms as this Article is being ratified.

Section 2

This article shall become inoperative unless it shall have ratified as an amendment to the Constitution by the legislatures of three fourths of the several states within seven years from the date of its submission to the States by the Congress.

AMENDMENT 23

Ratified March 29, 1961

Section 1:

The District constituting the seat of Government of the United States shall appoint in such manner as the Congress may direct

A number of electors of President and Vice President equal to the whole number of senators and Representatives in Congress to which the District would be entitled if it were a State, but in no event more than the least populous state; they shall be in addition to those appointed by the States but they shall be considered for the purposed of the election of President and Vice President to be electors appointed by a state and they shall meet in the District and perform such duties as provided by the 12th Article of Amendments.

Section 2:

Congress shall have the power to enforce this article by appropriate legislation.

AMENDMENT 24

Ratified January 23, 1964

Section 1

The right of the citizens of the United States to vote in any primary or other election for President or Vice President, for electors for President or Vice President, or for Senator or Representative in Congress, shall not be denied or abridged by the United States or any State by reason of failure to pay any poll tax or other tax.

Section 2

The Congress shall have power to enforce this article by appropriate legislation.

AMENDMENT 25

Ratified February 10, 1967

Section 1

In case of the removal of the President from office or of his death or resignation, the Vice President shall become President.

Section 2:

Whenever there is a vacancy in the office of the Vice President, the President shall nominate a Vice President who shall take office upon confirmation by a majority vote of both Houses of Congress

Section 3:

Whenever the President transmits to the President pro tempore of the Senate and the Speaker of the House of Representatives his written declaration that he is unable to discharge the powers and duties of his office, and until he transmits to them a written declaration to the contrary, such powers and duties shall be discharged by the Vice President as Acting President.

Thereafter, when the President transmits to the President pro tempore of the Senate and the Speaker of the House of Representatives his written declaration that no inability exists, he shall resume the powers and duties of his office unless the Vice President and a majority of either the principal officers of the executive department or such other body as Congress may by law provide, transmit within four days to the President pro tempore of the Senate and the Speaker of the House of Representatives their written declaration that the President is unable to discharge the powers and duties of his office. Thereupon Congress shall decide the issue, assembling within forty eight hours for that purpose if not in session. If the Congress within 21 days after receipt of the latter written declaration or if Congress determines by two thirds vote of both Houses that the President is unable to discharge the powers and duties of his office, the Vice President shall continue to discharge the same as Acting President; otherwise the President shall resume the powers and duties of his office.

AMENDMENT 26

Ratified July 1, 1971

Section 1:

The right of citizens of the United States who are eighteen years of age or older to vote shall not be denied or abridged by the United States or by any State on account of age.

Section 2:

The Congress shall have the power to enforce this article by appropriate legislation.

AMENDMENT 27

Ratified May 7, 1992

No law, varying compensation for the services of the Senators and Representatives shall take effect until an election of Representatives shall have intervened.

The history of this amendment and how the country got from a travel and stay over night stipend to what today is $175,000 to start for Congresspersons is very intriguing and more than likely something the PEOPLE did not consent to, which led to an amendment that those in "service" to the PEOPLE could not vote themselves a raise until a new House was elected, meaning those who voted in the raise could not get that raise until they were re-elected.

It is strongly recommended for every citizen to read the actual Constitution, Articles and Amendments, and keep them firmly in mind. The duties to keep these documents and their principles in full force are all of ours, not just those elected and paid to do so.

The next segments of this book are the actual shortened statements from The Manual of the United States Government. It is strongly recommended for every citizen to purchase copies of the current Manual of The United States Government, along with at least one Manual from the 1950's or 1960's and onward to see what changes were made, and if they were lawful changes. The Manual of The United States Government is available on the website of The National Archives, either electronically or for print purchase.

The Manual of The United States Government
THE Veteran's Administration

This section contains the agencies that were considered for main research topics for dissertation purposes. Following these sections will be the entire paraphrased, agency listing of The Manual of The United States Government (2004 and 2008).

The problems of the returning 9/11 Veterans, as well as the Veterans of previous United States wars being fully served as directed by the Manual of the United States Government (MUSG, 2004) are being investigated by Congress currently (Congress, 2012). The methods of investigative research are the proposed study for this research project. The question of whether accepted business methods may be compared to the studies currently being utilized. The differences will be examined by the use of a quantitative study of public perception of how the Veteran's Administration is performing and the perceived performance as illuminated by the research survey instrument compared to the available survey results from the VA itself.

The quantitative study of the expected gap between public perception of the duty and performance of a public agency compared to the duty and performance as found by a Congressional Investigation (Congress, 2006) is expected by the researcher to create an innovative assessment tool for public agency assessment for restructuring. The value of this study is to provide an efficient economic and time management tool for agencies to assess their performance annually. Preliminary research talking to clients, staff and administrators of the Veteran's Administration has indicated informally that the agencies do survey their staff, clients and management for reassessing studies. The follow up, indicated by informal discussions with clients, staff and management is that the surveys are not then utilized in the restructuring process.

Public perception surveys are a commonly used business method of reassessing an organization in preparation for strategic change design (Wren, 2994) (Cullen, Hughey, Kerr, 2006) (Carlos, 2006). The Manual of the United States Government (MUSG, 2004) and the Congressional Investigative Report of the Katrina Disaster of 2005 (Congress, 2006) will be used as comparison markers for the analysis of data obtained in a random survey of a diverse group of American citizens and residents. The survey instrument is designed to obtain public opinion as to the performance of a public agency. In the case of the Veteran's Administration there are current studies by Congressional Committees that will be added as they become available to compare the results of the survey statistics for perceived performance of the duty of the Veteran's Administration.

Agency Two-Bureau of Indian Affairs

The Bureau of Indian Affairs. There are many facets of the BIA and what it is legislated to accomplish. The first page of the discussion details the burden of duty enacted by the enabling legislation. The survey process was asking Native Americans how they feel the BIA is doing in meeting that duty. The comparison of the BIA's own performance reviews based on paperwork, rather than service and oversight was developed to show the need for straight forward performance review. Note: in preliminary survey test questions and personal interviews, Native Americans appear to not be educated in their rights, or the obligations of the treaties of the United States of America and their rights a dual citizens, of the United States of America, and their own Native Nations, this will be researched further in the research for the survey questions to include this aspect of the outcomes of the survey results.

The question making the most sense is simple: are Native Americans being serviced as guaranteed by the obligations of the Bureau of Indian Affairs in The Manual of the United States Government? The answer is somewhat complex: What is a Native American? WHO fits that definition to become a WHO? How do we answer the situations that are arising of people who are part non-Native? How doe we answer the situations of persons that are descended from two or more recognized nations? Once we have established who IS a Native American under the meaning of The Manual of The United States of America, the next questions are about what services are guaranteed.

The Manual of the United States of America states (MUSG, 2004; MUSG, 2008) under the Department of the Interior section, that the Office of the Assistant Secretary of Indian Affairs (BIA) is "responsible" directly supervising the Federal ...." Self-determination, self governance, gaming, ecnomic development, and ALL administrative, financial, and information resources management activities; and maintaining liaison and coordination between the Department and other Federal agencies that provide services...to Native Americans.

The stated mission of the Department of the Interior is "to protect and provide access to our Nation's natural and cultural heritage and honor our trust responsibilities to tribes and our commitments to island communities". First, these are nations, not tribes. It is demeaning to subjugate other nations and call them tribes when in fact they are NOT just nations, they are the original nations of the United States. Thomas Jefferson himself in his diaries and works declared that the systems of national interaction were where he formed some of his thoughts for the United States of America. Therefore, it must be argued that the burdens of the Manual of the United States Government must include the burdens of the treaties that brought the Native American Nations under the auspices of the Department of the Interior rather than the Department of State, or the military.

Further, the Office of the Special Trustee for American Indians (Native Americans) is stated to have the duty to: "oversee" "trust reform efforts department wide to ensure the establishment of policies, procedures, systems and practices to allow the Secretary to discharge the Government's fiduciary trust responsibilities to American Indians" (Native Americans) "and tribes" (Nations) (MUSG, 2008). Further, the Office has the responsibility for the management of financial trust assets, asset appraisals, and fiduciary trust beneficiary services".

These duties, enabled by Congress are clear that the BIA is intended to protect Native Americans, not sway at the whimsy of congresspersons, or lobbyists, or mining and cattle companies. At this point, the pipeline companies are also to be included, the Manual is clear that the DUTY of the United States is to PROTECT the Native Nations, NOT to take more land and assets away from the Native Nations or reduce treaty rights. Many, if not most of the reserves are recognized sovereign nations. The regulations of those nations can not be interfered with, there is absolutely NO statement of intent by the enabling Congress for the BIA to be used as a tool to further take rights, resources and assets or privileges away from Native Americans.

Looking at the reality of the 2010 settlements on the land trust misappropriations and poor management, it seems that the law involved came to the conclusion that these duties were NOT being met. However, the way in which those settlements were obtained might bring up other questions as the survey questions are contemplated. For example: a person who was not allowed to be a member of the class action due to the restrictions placed upon those allowed to recover was not open to discussion for settlement among the Natives of those nations. In many of the nations the chairman, or the law firm refused to fill out the paperwork necessary for the claims. This will be discussed after the survey results are tabulated and discussed.

Agency Three-Department of Homeland Security-FEMA

FEMA and the Department of Homeland Security. The question was suggested by a mentor, did FEMA improve its services from one fire/flood period in my local area to the same critical fire/flood period in the current year. I did not see this for any relevance to my original study, but have included the research in this work. For the book I have included the whole areas of FEMA and Homeland Security in light of recent critical events, not just one fire area.

Some years before 9/11 FEMA was founded to attempt to create faster, more focused disaster relief when necessary in any of the States or territories. The question overall in the surveys is did that work? Prior to FEMA each State had its own crisis response programs. Some still do, but others have simply given up the effort and joined Homeland Security, as FEMA was integrated into Homeland Security following 9/11.

Local counties and cities had their own disaster response and volunteer response units as well. In most areas these are no longer in place. One of the major disasters that illustrates the problems of this centralized, rather than widespread crisis response is the Montecito forest fires of 2010. Officially named The Tea Fires one of the most expensive and prestigious areas of Santa Barbara burned in essence before the fire fighters could arrive. The fire fighters live in an area about an hour and a half north of Santa Barbara, By the time they arrived, the fire had blown from the mountain to the ocean burning mansions in moments. Yet this researcher could not find one official paper in FEMA or in

Department of Homeland Security documents regarding remedies for the reality that fire personnel is no longer local volunteers, or local residents employed by the fire department. Even though media reports featured fire fighters who stated they could not afford to buy homes or live in the areas they were hired to protect created a reality that the fire fighters were not able to be available in less than 90 minutes to a fire that occurred off their assigned shift.

Agency Four- Department of Health and Human Services-Housing

Health and Human Services. Housing is a very broad issue, The Agency needs to have eraction with many other agencies, such as banking, insurance, and State and local vernments. The survey portion was kept simple, The question was, how is the agency meeting legislated duty, look around and see homeless persons, the duty is not being met.

Since I started this study, the foreclosure scandals have broken into public knowledge. e need for housing to be overseen by the agency that gives out billions of dollars on top of)se given by FEMA for disaster recovery, is evident in just headline stories on the internet and newspapers and magazines.

Agency Five-Department of Education, Department of Justice, Department of Health and Human Services-Equine Therapy Certification

The Department of Education, The Department of Health and Human Services and The Department of Justice in relation to the enabling legislation duties to provide children education, healthcare, safety, and justice are discussed as one unit. The survey was to talk to homeless, truant and abandoned youth and children. Just a few questions each. The goal was to show, as long as there are children homeless, truant and abandoned, the Departments are not meeting their duty. Health and Human Services has the duty to certify health programs for payment by insurance companies and hospitals or clinics. Equine therapy was the subject I chose, as it has been more than forty years that the therapy programs have been asking for certification to get paid.

The paper discusses the realities for the equine therapy programs and how they are working out the problems of not getting paid directly for services that are expensive. The paper also discusses the research showing the success rates of this type of therapy at a cost much lower in human suffering, and to the taxpayers for long term lock down treatment of many persons that have successfully completed the programs. The paper discusses some of the groups attempting to resolve these issues.

Additional Agencies. Thoughts,

In the first view, this book was going to just be the original five papers. In second thought, the book reduced the papers, except the first Chapter to a less formal discussion of the agency restructuring issues. This final chapter discusses remaining agencies in short. The goal is to reveal the enabling legislations of a variety of agencies and how they could be restructured to meet their goals rather than continue to add patches to the complex legislation that has failed the People of the United States of America. The end result is a complete set of agencies, as listed in the Manual of the United States Government 2008 version, with reassessment and restructuring suggestions based purely on the stated goals of the enabling Congress.

PRESIDENT-Executive Branch

The President although changes have been made, has strict Constitutional and Congressionally legislated mandates that cover what the President actually can do as President. This is not being elected King, Czar, or Dictator, nor is it being divinely admitted to royalty. Congress, and the Supreme Court both have duties assigned to them by the Founding and successive Congresses to assure that the President does not overstep, or fail to perform duties. In an older edition (2004) of the Manual, the President is described as the place where responsibility can not be passed. However, with that extreme duty, the President does NOT get the authority to do whatever he/she wants to. The People also have a power to assess the President and demand Congress to initiate an impeachment procedure if Congress finds upon investigation that the conditions are properly met to institute that proceeding. The conditions are very strict and precise as to what is an impeachable offense. ONLY The House of Representatives can bring an impeachment against a President. That House is held to very strict rules of what constitutes an impeachable offense, and the numbers of House of Representative members that must concur to bring the impeachment order to the Senate, the ONLY branch of government that can HEAR the case, the Justice of the Supreme Court is the only Judge able to hear an impeachment procedure.

CONGRESS

Although it can be argued that the United States Army was the first agency of the American Colonial resistance, it is not the first agency legally formed by the United States following the forming of the three branches of government designed by the Founders. The first agency listed is Congress. Created by the Founders of the United States of America in 1787, the first Congress did not convene until 1789. In slightly over 200 years Congress has had considerable changes which are discussed below in view of the past several years of serious flawed performance of Congress leading to the recent shut down of the whole United States Government (except for what were considered "essential services". The online discussions led the voters to question who decides what IS an essential service. Services for combat troops killed in action during the shut down were not considered essential until the voters and veterans groups protested and demanded that the return home and burial care WAS essential. Allowing the Nevada mustangs rounded up by Bureau of Land Management for slaughter to be alleged to have been left without water, except for small muddy puddles left by a fortunate rain storm was not essential. At the same time Congress had its gym reopened so they could have a sauna and workout. This infuriated the voters. An internet search of what constitutes "essential services" is something every voter needs to explore before voting again.

This leads to the conclusion that CONGRESS itself needs to be re-evaluated by a non-partisan commission, one that might be formed from all parties and independents to see where the changes were created, by whom and do the voters want these changes to remain. This could be a very short term research project for graduate students from several universities across the nation. Small research stipends would make this an in depth and inexpensive study. The committee would make recommendations for the voters to consider and a Bill would be created to present to the voters across the nation in the next national election.

During the years since the death of President Kennedy there have been numerous changes that it appears may not be either legal changes, or in the best interest of the people of the United States of America. Many documents have been declassified, which would give the committee and the voters a more comprehensive view of the realities of the situations regarding Congress. It is the duty of citizens to know these facts before they vote for any politician.

It would be within the admonitions of Benjamin Franklin for the voters to demand this type of committee review of Congress itself in view of the crisis in economic and employment and other areas of governance that need to be investigated and the problems resolved. The failure of Congress after Congress to have a budget on the date it is due, or to make that a balanced budget, the exceptional debt, and spending beyond the budget limits all rest on how Congress is functioning as an agency. The People, in Benjamin Franklin's views could also demand investigations by the Supreme Court, and/ or the Executive Branch of the government of Congress. These oversight tools were put into our founding documents to assure the People would have tools to regain control from a runaway Congress, which this past month appears to be the argument of many of the citizens. The argument can be strongly made that if the founders meant for Congress to just take off and do whatever it wanted.......they would not have incorporated a three leveled governmental system of checks and balances. It would also appear that Ben Franklin and others would not have put into the Declaration of Independence the DUTY as well as RIGHT of the PEOPLE to keep constant vigil and control over government.

THE GOVERNMENT ACCOUNTABILITY OFFICE

This agency is interesting in view of Presidents since the first President Bush, Vice President Al Gore, and President Bush and now Obama working on systems which have given us the EBT cards, not just for food stamps, general relief and other welfare payments, Medicare and Medicaid cards, but also a form of EBT card put into contention by Vice President Al Gore for use of the entire budget to cut corruption and waste in the government. (President Clinton is not mentioned because the research data stated the project was turned over to Vice President Al Gore, with no fact as to whether is was just his idea, or that of the President as well).

This agency has as its enabling legislated duty to investigate matters relating to the receipt and disbursement of federal funds. Vice President Al Gore's use of EBT type of systems took checks out of the system for many programs. Some checks were given to large agencies, for disbursal, other checks were given to States for disbursal to their State agencies as indicated in the budget agreements for the enabling legislative use of the funds. The use of earmarks on Congressional legislation created a way for money to be sidetracked from an appropriation.......for something that has nothing to do with the Bill being passed just being added on. One famous earmark was a couple of million dollars added in to a budget on a Bill for something else that in the end led to what amounted to a personal gift from a Congressperson to his Auntie for her tea pot museum hobby (Rick Santorum as reported in Politifacts 2012). Another tea pot museum was also awarded an earmark of $400,000 in another Politifacts report of 2007), the earmarking Congressperson noting it was such a nice museum it deserved funds. WE as a nation NEED oversight on our hard earned taxpayer money.

The EBT card system also would have ended the practice of "losing" large checks. Especially States were prone to "losing" large federal checks. The counties, cities, hospitals, police departments, fire departments, and juvenile and family programs just went without waiting for those checks to be found. One check I had experience with was for $13 Million dollars for a county juvenile program. The block grant applications were given out, people had leased buildings, hired staff......the checks never came down from the State. More than a year later, the State notified the county that they had "found" the money...but returned it to the Federal government due to the time passing....no mention of the float on that $13 million dollars. The programs were all closed and many had been sued by employees and landlords. But someone, somewhere, had what may have been almost one million dollars of float on that money.

With the EBT card system, the money would have gone directly to the counties, cities and agencies, as the budgets indicated. Every payment would have been released to the vendor, upon the proper electronic signatures, the funds never leaving the taxpayer protected account until released to the end vendor or agency for payroll or benefit distribution. Every single penny would have been traceable at any time of any day. As can be seen by the above small example, a "lost" check for several billion dollars could create a large amount of float in a short amount of time. That is in reality money embezzled from the American taxpayers.

Another utilization of the GAO that would have benefited the taxpayers would be the Federal budget. Since the money would NEVER go anywhere, the IRS collections would all be daily record, and the budget amount expected would have been available as soon as the IRS filings were completed and balanced each year. Any funds from other sources, mandatory fees, etc, would have been in one account by wire transfer each day and therefore completely transparent and up to date. This would have given the GAO a daily transparent record of where the money from the taxpayers came from and where it was going.

The oversight of these suggested programs to taxpayer funds was also inclusive of funds in States that had to be reported and given proper oversight before a State could apply for any grant, or bond relief from the Federal Government. Note: These proposed systems would have made EVERY store, every gambling establishment, every ein number have DAILY reports that are easily electronically generated and followed that would have increased the budgets and reduced taxes. Every State would have to report ALL their fees, fines, penalties and lottery and other income DAILY to IRS ,this would have been a one page Bill that would simplify and make transparent ALL taxpayer money in and out. States and local governments would have to do these electronic filing each day before midnight their own time zone would be required to do this to file a request for ANY Federal funds.

The mission statement of the GAO includes the duty to determine if every agency or branch of government is doing the job it is assigned to do within the enabling legislation voted in by the Congress that formed that agency or branch of government.

This would indicate that the Founders of the GAO intended for an annual, accurate investigation and oversight be provided to the People of where their money was coming from and going to in meeting the goals their Congress had put in place. The President appears in the 2004 edition of the Manual of the Untied States Government to have been given the duty to oversee that all branches and agencies were in compliance with their enabling legislation.

The addition of duty to oversee financial concerns of the PEOPLE creates the DUTY of the President to make sure that a system is developed and implemented that better oversees the funding, and use of public funds.

CONGRESSIONAL BUDGET OFFICE

The Congressional Budget Office was established in 1974. This office provides Congress with ALL that it needs to have a complex and complete budget forecast, as well as investigations and reports on specific areas of the budget and fiscal policy issues. In 1995 an additional amendment was added to the Congressional Budget Office duties, that of making sure that any mandate for more than five years of unfunded duties would be required of the Congressional Budget office. The establishment of this Office gives a taxpayer some question to the compliance of both the Office and the Congress on budget issues. The Congressional Budget Office it would appear has was given the job to facilitate the annual budget for the United States of America. One wonders whether this Office is failing to produce mandatory documentation and forecasts to give Congress no excuse for not getting the budget done in a timely and efficient manner each year. The oversight on this office, as well as Congress on budget appears in the mandatory duties of this Office to be simple. IF there is no budget, or the budget is not appropriate to the forecast of the previous Office documentation: investigation would seem to be appropriate to resolve the problems of budgets that have plagued the United States of America these past few decades.

The application of the 1995 amendment on mandates that are unfunded for at least five years would appear to address the Affordable Healthcare Act issues that have been tried over and over in the media. It would appear from the wording on page 61 of the 2008 Manual of The United States Government that the Congressional Budget Office should have been doing investigations and preparing the reports to Congress regarding the direct costs of the Act. It might be wondered by the taxpayers, if this Office was doing its job, rather than Congresspersons attempting over and over to defund, or undermine a mandate that had passed. This would have freed up Congress to resolve issues of the taxpayers and citizens, rather than to continue a tiresome back and forth on a mandate that had been passed. If, as appears to be occurring, the Act began to unravel and cost more money than affordable, the suggested annual review would give Congress a well supported research report each year to work with to investigate how to salvage health CARE rather than mandatory insurance that is in contention.

It might also be wondered it the Congressional Budget Office should not have investigated and filed reports on the costs of the War in Iraq, and War in Afghanistan, and the many secret military actions and private contractor expenditures that are not included transparently in other budget reports. The Congressional Budget Office appears to be an Office giving the specific duty of the preparation and suggestions of alternative fiscal policies. In a working financial division of a successful company it would seem prudent to have an office that makes sure the money will fit the income. It might be wondered if this is not the duty given to the Congressional Budget Office.

JUDICIAL: SUPREME COURT

The judicial power of the United States of America says the Constitution, quoted in the mandate statement of the Supreme Court of The United States of America in the Manual of the United States Government, IS the Supreme Court of the United States of America. Created in 1789 it was made an Article of the Constitution on February 2, 1790. The Supreme Court has a Supreme Court Chief Justice and a number of Associate

Justices as legislated by Congress. At the writing of the 2008 Manual of the United States of America, that number was eight (28.U.S.C.1) and remains the same currently.

An interesting statement of the Manual of the United States Government (page 68, 2008) is that Congress has NO power to change the jurisdiction of the Supreme Court. This would seem to negate many a political advertisement and argument that allows that Congress does have power to enlarge or diminish the jurisdiction of the Supreme Court. The Court itself was given the power to establish lower courts, and has maintained the appellate power for itself. The Supreme Court has the power to simply refuse to hear a case, although it gives a legal reason for such refusal, which may be contested, to the Supreme Court itself by addressing the issues raised by the Supreme Court for refusing to hear the appeal. The Supreme Court on its own decision can hear cases or not as they see a Constitutionally appropriate case. The Supreme Court can make decisions based on both fact and law, BUT, the Supreme Court can NOT legislate through Court findings. The Supreme Court MAY consider precedent setting cases, OR not, in making a finding on a particular issue. The political myth that Justices can be appointed to change legislation is based on unsound practice which Congress DOES have the power to investigate and impeach justices if it can be proven they are acting in an illegal use of the powers of The Supreme Court.

LOWER COURTS

As for the Supreme Court, Congress and the Court may establish lower courts, as the Court sees fit, some of which may be for a special short term issue if formed to be so. As with the Supreme Court, these lower court judges cannot be removed except for other than "good behavior". The Constitution and interpretations have created the reality that Lower Court justices, and Supreme Court justices can NOT be removed by Congress, or the President or even the taxpayers on a whimsical dispute of issues or party philosophies. A President, or Congress that is of another party has no power to remove a justice unless "good behavior" is no longer shown. Even then the person wanting the justice removed has to follow Constitutional procedure and is bound by those in the position to implement the process and actual removal of a justice.

In the Manual of the United States Government, 2008, it is clearly stated that Congress has NO power to remove justices for anything other than a failure to maintain "good behavior". This has NEVER been interpreted as a dispute in the findings of a Court and the desires of the Congress in a certain case or issue.

The United States Courts of Appeals were established in March 1891 to relieve the Supreme Court of the burden of the number of appeals being brought. Today a matter MAY be brought directly to the Supreme Court, but most often it will be sent back for initial hearing by the appropriate Court of Appeals. There is a protocol of appeals for matters brought before the Supreme Court and the Court of Appeals.

One Court that has been added in 1982 is the United States Court of Appeals for the Federal Circuit. This Court is located in Washington DC and deals with patents and delineated business customs laws. It replaced the previous United States Court of Customs and Patent Appeals. This Court has jurisdiction over the nation and territories for all established cases in Patents and certain contracts and civil actions in which the United States is a party in the matter. This Court oversees other special courts that handle a long list of matters that are specialized and have large bodies of law pertaining to just the one area of law which involve the United States of America.

One example is the Court that handles Veterans matters. The oversight of these Courts is assigned to the justices of the Supreme Court. Each court has 12 justices and sits in panels of three, however it may sit in full panel of all 12 justices should the justices or the Supreme Court decide to do so in a particular case. While the home of the Court is in Washington DC, the cases may be heard wherever there is a court of appeals (28 U.S.C.48).

The United States District courts and the Territorial Courts are the trial courts for the Federal jurisdiction. Each Court has from 2 to 26 justices depending on the level of work being done in the District. Most cases are heard by one judge, but a limited number of cases require three judges (28 U.S.C. 2284). An appeal, if applied for is sent to the United States of Appeals for filing and if necessary may be appealed to the Supreme Court for consideration. The Supreme Court is not mandated to hear any case, and may on its own motion send any part, or all of a case back to the lower court for further investigation or findings. There is a Judicial Panel on Multidistrict Litigation that since 1968 ((23 U.S.C.1407) can be convened with seven Judges rather than to expect either party in a case to attempt to file in several affected Districts separately.

The checks and balances provided by these Court systems and appeals create a system to facilitate an issue being heard fairly. The judges do not like being reversed and knowing that appeals are going to be based on reversible errors and findings by them, the judges are more deeply involved in keeping the cases and findings bound by law, rather than any other reason. Political, economic, or personal belief are easier to leave outside of court rulings when another, higher Court holds the right to oversight through appeals. The method of judges being selected or elected gives the People an opportunity to support, or protest a judge being on a certain Court, or case.

A complaint to the Supreme Court is taken into consideration if the Court decides there is merit to the complaint regarding unethical, or corrupted performance by any justice or employee in the Supreme Court system. This is a valuable tool to the continued balanced and ethical court performance, again, if justices, lawyers, and employees know they can, and will be investigated upon complaint, it is supportive to their rendering of the jobs entrusted to them by the People. This is another of the balances built into our system to empower the People to oversee the Courts.

SPECIAL COURTS

There are special courts mandated from time to time by a Congress to create the Judicial balancing arm of the three branches of the United States Government ability to work more efficiently. One of these Courts is the United States Court of Federal Claims. A complaint for money damages against the United States itself must be a claim based on the Constitution giving a basis for the claim, an act of Congress having created the enabling legislation to create a duty for the claim to be based upon, or an order arising from an executive department that created the base of the claim. The final area of these claims that can only be heard in the U.S. Court of Federal Claims is from express or implied in fact contracts with the United States. These do not include tort, only contract issues. The Justices for this Court are appointed whenever there is a vacancy created by death, retirement, or resignation of a Justice. Each Justice may serve for 15 years. The Senate must confirm the appointments. Appeals from this Court are to the U.S. Court of Appeals for the Federal Circuit. The requirement of a Senate confirmation gives the voters an opportunity to voice their opinion on the nomination and confirmation as the residents of a State can refuse to support, or vote for that Senator again if the demands of the voters in that State are not considered in the confirmation process.

An important issue in these Courts is that the Justices be fairly chosen to decide LAW, not on the side of lobbyists who are pushing the Senators to put justices in place that will serve the wants of those who want to take land and assets from another State or territory against contracts made by the United States to protect those States and Territories against being over run by outside monopolists and lobbyists.

THE UNITED STATES COURT OF APPEALS FOR THE ARMED FORCES

The United States Court of Appeals for the Armed Forces is another Special Court. This Court of Appeal was established in 1950 by an amendment to the Constitution (10 U.S.C.867). This Court is only subject to a limited review of the United Supreme Court if appeal is requested. The judges are five civilian judges, appointed for 15 year terms by the President of the United States of America. The jurisdiction of this Court is to review cases involving death sentences, sentences over one year certified by a Judge Advocate General of the armed forces, Department of Transportation Advocates, or Coast Guard Court Justices. A punitive discharge may be appealed to this Court.

These Justices are required by their initiating legislation to make an annual report to Congress on the operation and progress of the United States military justice system. This report is to include recommendations for improvement in the military justice system.

UNITED STATES TAX COURT

Another Special Court is the United States Tax Court. This Court was established under Article I of the Constitution of the United States of America (26 U.S.C.7441). This Court has a long history of name changes and duties. In 1924, eleven years after the formal establishment of income tax as a duty of residents of the United States of America the initial United States Tax Court was named the United States Board of Tax Appeals, which was an independent branch of the legislative branch of government. By 1969 the name United States Tax Court was established (83 Stat. 730).

The current United States Tax Court allows the taxpayer to take an option for a faster, specialized Court to hear tax matters under $50,000(title 26 U.S. Code). These lesser Courts, if opted for, have no appeal benefit. Cases larger than $50,000 for any one tax year must be heard in the United States Tax Court under the provisions of title 26 of the tax codes. Any case heard in the United States Tax Court may request an appeal process from the Federal Court of Appeals, and if necessary may petition the Supreme Court under the provisions of the law.

THE UNITED STATES COURT OF APPEALS FOR VETERANS CLAIMS

The United States Court of Appeals for Veterans Claims originally named the United States Court of Veterans Appeals which was established in 1988 (102 Stat. 4105, U.S.C 7251) under Constitutional provisions of Article I of the Constitution to review decisions of the Board of Veterans Appeals. Renamed United States Court of Appeals for Veterans Claims in 1998 in the Veterans Programs Enhancement Act of 1998 (38 U.S.C 7251). The Court was prohibited from reviewing schedules of ratings and actions of the Secretary of the Veteran's Administration in adopting or revising a schedule. These schedules are proposed and adopted by Congress. Seven judges serving 15 year terms are appointed by the President. One of the judges serves as the chief judge.

COURT OF APPEALS FOR THE DISTRICT OF COLUMBIA

There are other special courts, a local Court of Appeals for the District of Columbia, and the Superior Court. These Courts are described in detail annually in the Annual Report of the Director of the Administrative Office of the United States Courts. From time to time a special Court may be appointed by the Supreme Court which would also be described in detail in the years that special Court was functioning in the Annual Report of the Director of the Administrative Office of the United States Courts.

THE ADMINISTRATIVE OFFICE OF THE UNITED STATES COURTS

The Administrative office of the United States courts was created in 1939 by the Justices following a Judicial Conference (28 U.S.C. 601) in which the charge was given for non-judicial aspects of the United States Courts separate from the duties of the Justices on the various Courts have an administrative office. The duties of the Administrative office include administration of the Courts, maintenance of records for the Courts, including workload statistics and other records necessary for the Annual Report of the Courts which must be submitted to Congress. The Administrative Office of the United States Courts also deals with disbursements of funds appropriated for the court system.

Courts that also are included in the duties of the Administrative Office of he United States Courts are Bankruptcy, Federal Magistrate Judge Court records and disbursements and the oversight of Federal probation officers. The statistics and records are also compiled and submitted with the Annual United States Courts Report to Congress to facilitate Congress being able to have on hand current information to create budget and appropriations decisions for the following year for the Supreme Court System of the United States of America.

FEDERAL JUDICIAL CENTER

The Federal Judicial Center was created by Congress in 1967 (28 U.S.C.621) to improve and develop the Courts of the United States of America. This center is the judicial branch's agency for policy research and to maintain and create continuing education for all levels of the Federal Court systems.

The Chief Justice of the Supreme Court is always a member of the Board of the Federal Judicial Center. A grouping of judges was established in the enabling legislation that as of the Manual of the United States Government (2008) consisted of two U.S. Court of appeals judges, three judges of the U.S. district court, one bankruptcy judge and one magistrate judge all whom are elected for four year terms at the Judicial Conference of the United States. The Director of the Administrative Office of the United States Courts is another required Board member.

There are five specified duties of the Federal Justice Center:

- Develop and administer orientation and continuing education programs for all judges and employees of the Federal Court system
- Conducts empirical and exploratory research and evaluation of Federal judicial process, court management and sentencing and he consequences. This work is usually done at the request of the Judicial Conference itself
- Produces the research reports, training manuals, broadcasts, video, compute based online programs and periodicals for the Federal Court system
- Provides guidance and advice. Maintains data and records to assist those interested in documenting and conserving the history of the Federal Judiciary and the Courts
- Cooperates and assists other agencies and organizations in providing advice to improve the administration of justice in foreign countries.

UNITED STATES SENTENCING COMMISSION

The sentencing reform act of f1984 created a commission to assist in producing policies and guidelines that would establish a consistent guideline for justices and judges to follow.

EXCUTIVE BRANCH:
PRESIDENT

The President of the United States of America was never designed to be a ruler, but instead a servant. Like Congress, and the Courts, the Founders of America wrote every single work of the Constitution with long argument and gave careful thought to how the ONLY governing document of the United States of America was worded. The Manual of the United States Government contains the most elementary of the legislations that added or amended duties of any of the three branches of our government. The Constitution is very clear that every single member of any branch is to be OF, BY and FOR the People. The oaths of office are worded to forward this duty to SERVE rather than to rule.

Article II, section 1, of the Constitution sets forth the powers and responsibilities of the President of the United States. The Manual previously contained the words (from President Roosevelt) that The President of the United States of America had the SOLE, final resting duty to assure that NO PERSON on American soil suffered poverty or the results of poverty. It has been removed. The words put in its place are "The President is the administrative head of the executive branch of the Government" and goes on to detail that includes numerous agencies, both temporary and permanent. There is no indication of how or who, or why it was removed. Regardless of removing those words, the Constitution of the United States of America puts the burden of each duty of Administrating on the President of the United States, clearly as a servant, not a tyrant, monarch, or despot of any description.

The Cabinet is at the pleasure of the President going back to George Washington and is designed to be an advisory group . At present there are 15 Secretaries (Manual of United States Government, 2008). (Article II, section 2 of the Constitution). Each Cabinet member is expected to oversee anything pertinent to the cabinet position to answer and support the President or Vice President with advice and information when requested.

Note as of July 2017: There has been a lot of problems in America regarding the selection and/or removal of advisors. The Manual of The United States Government is clear that these are ADVISORY positions at the PLEASURE of the President. As seen in The Manual of the United States Government as current as 2008, the sentence regarding the pleasure of the President, and the advisory only categorization of these Cabinet members is still in use, as it was since the time of President George Washington......The Cabinet are NOT elected, and have NO power other than to ADVISE the President, Congress and Supreme Court. Even Agencies that are enabled by legislation are NOT able to over rule the Constitution and the three branches of elected government. While the Supreme Court is not elected, it has been chosen for the most part from justices who have been elected and confirmed into positions by elected representatives as required by the Constitution.

VICE PRESIDENT

Article II, section 1 of the Constitution provides the law to govern the Office of the Vice President of The United States of America. The Vice President is the President of the Senate. Additional duties of the Vice President are: To be able at any moment to step into the Presidency, temporarily or for the remainder of a term of office when the President dies or is unable to serve, in addition to attend cabinet meetings, and by statute have membership on the National Security Council and for the Board of Regents of the Smithsonian Institute.

The People of the United States of America need to be clear on the election of a Vice President, this is not just a second chair, this may become the duty bound servant of the Office of the President of The United States of America. A careful study of history has shown some serious errors have occurred in the selection of Vice Presidents who did in fact become President.

It is imperative for the voters to KNOW who they have elected for positions that may put them into the office of the Presidency. However, Benjamin Franklin in particular told the People, over and over that safeguards were written into the founding documents of the United States of America to protect against tyrants and would be emperors. One of these is impeachment and the right for citizens to demand a President be recalled. The terms of office protect the People from empire builders and tyrants as well. The Constitution allows only four years between elections, and includes the impeachment tool for Presidents, or Vice Presidents the People feel have deserved to be impeached. Later Amendments limited the number of terms a President may serve in the office of President.

EXECUTIVE OFFICE OF THE WHITE HOUSE;

OFFICE OF THE PRESIDENT

The Office of the President, is not the President. The Office was created in a reform act of 1939, which created the Executive Office of the President and was established by the President's Reorganization Plans I and II of 1939 (5 U.S.C app.) Executive Order 8248 established the divisions of that Office of the President and established the functions of each position. Each President has added amendments as necessary to meet their administrative goals.

One of the main duties of this Office is to keep the Administration moving smoothly and seamlessly from President to President. To maintain communication with Congress, heads of agencies, the press, media and the People, the persons the Constitution guarantees will be served, not ruled. The President may add or decrease positions to meet current work goals. President Kennedy was said to have read ALL of his mail, it was of course opened, and sorted, but of the normal letters from constituents, he was said to read them all, make little notes and have them answered, this would seem to have been possible with his incredible reading skills. President Clinton too was said to read his sorted mail and make small notes to those that required an answer. Most Presidents rely on the Executive Office of the President to open, sort, and categorize all mail. Some few letters are given to the President, the rest are sent to units or groups as the staff decides is best to handle the issues raised in the letters. Presidential paperwork and items that will one day be of interest to the Presidential Library are also under the auspices of the Office of the President staff assigned to that task.

OFFICE OF THE VICE PRESIDENT

Similar to the Executive Office, the Office of the Vice President was established to handle the Administrative duties of the Vice President. As with the President, paperwork that needs to be kept for historical or government business is kept by the staff of this office.

COUNCIL OF ENVIRONMENTAL ADVISERS

Established by the Executive Office of the President by the Employment Act of 1946 (15 U.S.C.1023), but has been restructured by statute and the Reorganization Plan No. 9, 1953 (5 U.S. C. app). The Council is a three member (as of the 2008 Manual of the United States of America) who are appointed by the President and confirmed by the Senate at the time of appointment nomination. The President appoints, or designates who is the President of the Council. With no real political power, these members are expected to keep abreast of economics in the United States and in relation to the global economy and advise the President. This council prepares the annual report on the economy to the President and the Congress in all areas of programs, policies of the Federal Government economy and provides an ongoing analysis of the nations economy.

COUNCIL ON ENVIRONMENTAL QUALITY

The Council on environmental quality formulates and recommends national policies that promote improvement of the quality of the environment. The council was formed in 1969 (4 U.S.C.4321) as many concerns about the environment began to reach a critical level and the citizens demanded more Federal involvement in many areas of environmental policies and controls. In 1970 The Environmental Quality Improvement

Act *42 U.S.C. 4371) provided professional and administrative support to the Council and gave the Council more power to create and mandate policies to evaluate, coordinate, and advise environmental issues into policies and mandates for advice suggestions to the Executive branch. This Council also oversees and implements National Environmental Protection Act provisions and mandates.

National Security Council

This office was established in 1947 (50 U.S.C. 402) and placed in the Executive Office of the President by the Reorganization Act of 1949 (5 U.S.C. app.). Later discussions of this Council and departments and divisions of the National Security Act have come under scrutiny as President Truman, who signed the Act into being, has since in his autobiographies said he made a "mistake" by creating what he deemed "secret government". Again, Franklin gave us clues, specifically for this type of "error" or even aggressively traitorous legislation that creates any council or department, or legislator and made sure fail safe clauses were put in to give citizens, and legislators the ability to investigate and change, or recall laws that give citizens the tools for change.

OFFICE OF ADMINISTRATION

The Office of administration was established in 1977, by Executive Order 12028 to provide administrative support services to all units within the Presidents Executive office, this included information, technology, financial management, data processing, library and research services, security, legislative liaisons, and the general office operations, which include mail, messenger, printing, procurement and supply services.

OFFICE OF MANAGEMENT AND BUDGET

The Office of Management and Budget (OMB) was formerly the Bureau of Budget, re-established in the Executive Office of the President in the Reorganization Plan No 1 of 1939. The OBM evaluates, formulates and coordinates management procedures and program objectives with and among Federal agencies and departments. This is the formal description of the OBM which will be discussed at length further in this book. The OBM routinely provides the President with recommendations regarding budget proposals and relevant legislative enactments. The Budget of the United States Government and The Budget System and Concepts of the United States Government are two annual publications of the OBM available upon request to the Superintendent of Documents at the Government Printing Office, Washington D.C. 20401.

OFFICE OF NATIONAL DRUG CONTROL POLICY

Established in 1988 The Office of National Drug Control Policy was created by the National Narcotics Leadership act (21 U.S.C. 1501 et seq.) effective January 29,1989. The office duties were amended in the 1994 Violent Crime Control and Law Enforcement Act (21 U.S.C. 1502, 1506, 1508) and again reauthorized by the Office of National Drug Control Reauthorization Act of 2006 (21 U.S.C. 1701 note). The Director is appointed by the President and is assisted by Deputies in many areas of drug policy and control. The Office of National Drug Control Policy is responsible for establishing policies, objective, priorities, and performance measurement for the national drug control program. Annual reports and financial budget reviews are submitted to the President of the United States and to Congress by the Director of the Office.

OFFICE OF POLICY DEVELOPMENT

This office includes the Assistant to the President for Domestic Policy, and the Deputy Assistant to the President for Domestic Policy as well as the Assistant to the President for Economic Policy and the Director of National Economic Policy and his Deputy Director. Utilizing the Offices that create reports and budgets, this office is to assist the President in developing domestic,economic policies. Developed in 1993 by Executive Order 12859 the Domestic Policy Council oversees the development and implementation of the Presidents domestic policy agenda. The council coordinates and communicates with the heads of the relevant Federal offices and agencies on each policy to assure it is implemented efficiently and in a timely manner.

The National Economic Council was also established in 1993 by Executive Order 12835 to coordinate the communications; implementation of economic policymaking processes and provide advice to the President to keep the stated goals consistent with the ongoing economic policies.

OFFICE OF SCIENCE AND TECHNOLOGY POLICY

The Office of Science and Technology Policy was established by the National Science and Technology Policy, Organization and Priorities Act of 1976 (42 U.S.C. 6611). The Office serves to keep the President supplied with science and technology reports, analysis, policy recommendations, plans and programs for the Federal Government Science and Technology policies. This office also advises the President in providing leadership and development of programs in areas related to the Office of Budget Management related to these programs.

OFFICE OF THE UNITED STATES TRADE REPRESENTATIVES

The Office of the United States Trade Representatives for Trade Negotiations was established by Executive Order 11075 in 1963. The Trade act of 1974 (19 U.S.C. 2171) established the Office as an agency of the Executive Office of the President. This Office was created to administrate trade agreements programs. The Office is responsible for setting and administering overall trade policies. The Chief trade representative is expected to administrate the General Trade Agreement on Tariffs and Trade, oversee all meetings discussions and negotiations in the Organization for Economic Cooperation and Development that deal with trade and commodities. The chief administrator also is responsible for all negotiations in the UN conference on Trade and Development that deal with trade and commodities, as well as other East /West trade of commodities. Included in the duties are negotiations under 704 and 734 of the Tariff Act of 1930 (19

U.S.C. 1671 and 1673) and negotiations regarding direct investment as direct and indirect barriers to bilateral investment issues.

The Office is headed by a Cabinet level chief with the rank of an Ambassador, directly responsible to the President. There are three deputies to the chief who also hold the rank of Ambassador, Two located in Washington DC and one in Geneva, the Chief of Agricultural Trade also holds the rank of Ambassador. The Chief Administrator serves as an ex officio member of the Boards of Directors of the Export-Import Bank and the Overseas Private Investment Corporation, as well as the National Advisory Council for the International Monetary and Financial Policy.

As the United States has grown from the original 13 States, the need for advisors who know their fields and can be trusted by the Executive Branch has grown. Some of the positions include Board seats on other councils or agencies to ensure that the President has a criss cross of information to assure his best knowledge on subject within the jurisdiction of the Executive Branch, and to enable the President to fulfill the priority job of the President of the United States, which is, as stated above, the primary responsibility to see that ALL the residents are served within the demands and assigned duties of the Constitution of the United States of America. Each of these councils and administrators relies heavily on the agencies that have been established over the history of the United States of America to provide the Executive Branch with ongoing and up to date oversight of the areas listed below:

EXECUTIVE AGENCIES:

The Executive Agencies are there to advise the President and the Councils related to their functions, budgets, programs and critical issues. Each of these Executive Agency is created to make sure that as the United States of America grows, there are appropriate oversights to guarantee the residents and trade nations of the services covered under the mandates of Acts of Congress that regulate each area. The three branches of the government may have their own committees, councils, advisors, but all must file an annual (or monthly if mandated, daily for some agencies) report that can be used by the appropriate councils and Congress and the Courts to have immediate access to knowledge necessary for their work, and for creating policy based on reality. One of the reasons for the initial study in reassessing and restructuring public agencies was to explore and research the oversight, and communications between these agencies to make sure they all serve the persons the Constitution guarantees will be served by any government elected, appointed, or hired agency person or team. This aspect is explored at length in later discussions. The definitions below are from The Manual of The United States Government (2008) to establish the real law under which each of these agencies was legislated, and the mandates for their performance. This aspect too will be discussed at length in later chapters. It is deeply suggested that EVERY taxpayer and voter have a copy of THE Manual of the United States Government and follow the practices of the agencies and their interaction with politicians running for office, or in office. Our government IS a government OF the PEOPLE, BY the PEOPLE and FOR the PEOPLE, the PEOPLE therefore have a duty to know the government and oversee its activities.

AGRICULTURE

In the 2008 volume of The Manual of The United States Government, the editorial note at the beginning of the chapter is that the Department of Agriculture could not meet its mandate under the Freedom of Information Act (5 U.S.C. 552 (a)(1)(A)) to provide the required updated information of activities, functions, and sources of information. This is a serious failure of the part of any Department or Agency. The Constitution itself guarantees, and the amendments and statutes have strengthened the right of THE people (Of, By and For the PEOPLE) to know what those hired to work in their behalf are doing, how the money is being spent, and who is supplying information that results in policy decisions. This problem of failures within government to give respect and priority to the Constitution as creating barriers to open and appropriate governance by any of the three branches of government will be discussed in later chapters as it relates to reassessing and restructuring public agencies.

The MANDATE for the Department of Agriculture is to improve and maintain farm income. TO develop and expand markets abroad. To curb and cure poverty as related to nutrition, hunger and malnutrition. The Department of Agriculture has a MANDATE to enhance the environment and maintain production capacity by protection of soil, water, forests and other natural resources. The development of rural credit, production and conservation programs are listed as being KEY to carrying out national growth policies. The Department is MANDATED to supply research that directly or indirectly benefits ALL Americans. Through inspection and grading services, safeguards and making an assurance that standards of the food industry quality are set and met.

The Department of Agriculture was created in 1862 (7 U.S.C. 2201. The Department relies on support of Office of Chief Financial Officer, Office of Communications, Office of Congressional and Intergovernmental Relations, Office of the Inspector General and Office of General Counsel in performance of the tasks assigned to the Department by the enabling legislation.

The United States Department of Agriculture has its own sub-offices:

The Office of Rural Development is to increase both the quality of life of rural Americans and their business opportunities. New cooperatives between Government, industry and communities are fostered and developed by the Office of Rural Development. This includes a capital investment bank to provide housing and community facilities, business and cooperative development, telephone and internet access, electric, water and sewer infrastructures for rural homes and small farms. The loan and grant programs are operated from approximately 800 field offices to accomplish the goals of the Department. The guaranteed loans may be used for real property, working capital, machinery and equipment, buildings, and certain kinds of debt refinancing.

The Business Enterprise grants are available to facilitate obtaining of grants for public bodies, nonprofit corporations, and programs on Federally recognized Native American reserves, or for groups of their members in rural business enterprises. Business Opportunities division promotes sustainable business in rural areas. Renewable energy

and efficiency loans and grants are available for rural areas to sustain and attract
population.

The Co-op programs and development are large segments of the Department to
encourage small farmers to network to allow them to build more sustainable communities
and businesses in rural areas. The Department has established a Cooperative
Opportunities and Problems Research division to encourage research in critical areas to
the sustainability of agriculture. Business Opportunities is designed to promote
sustainable business in rural areas. Other grant areas are renewable energy, and efficiency
systems for areas of agriculture and sustainable rural life support programs. Electric and
telecommunications systems if eligible can borrow money or get loans to increase
services to rural areas. Especially if these businesses or systems are creating new job
opportunities, or increasing medical, dental and elder care they are encouraged by the
Economic Development division of the Department of Agriculture.

Intermediary re-lending programs are encouraged if properly approved for
community development projects that may need support to get loans in rural areas. The
National Sheep Industry Improvement Centers promote strategic plans for sheep farmers.
Rural housing, rural utilities, including water, heating fuels, energy, sewage control and
trash control and recycling are all areas that are eligible to apply for Department of
Agriculture loans and grants under their Economic Division programs. The programs
include advisors that can help rural cooperatives and city groups upgrade their quality of
life and food production for the nation.

Marketing and Regulatory Programs of the Department of Agriculture were
designed to assist farmers in areas other than food safety which is another division and
works with food and drug and other agencies to protect the nation's food resources.
Agricultural Marketing Service was established in 1972 in the Reorganization Plan No. 2
of the 1953 Agricultural legislation (5 U.S.C. app.). This division regulates
standardization, grading, certification, market news, marketing orders, research and
promotion to facilitate farmers being able to sell food to the nation and consumers,

wholesalers, and food production companies to have standardized systems and expectation of quality.

Animal and Plant Health Inspection Service is an important division of the Department of Agriculture, established in 1977 by 5 U.S.C. 301 and the Reorganization Plan 2 of 1953 (5 U.S.C. app.). This is one of the most visible divisions of the Department of Agriculture, the one responsible for the health and humane treatment of the animals and plants. This division will be discussed at length below.

Biotechnology Regulatory Services. This is another division that will be discussed at length below, Established in the same block of the 1977 additions to the 1953 legislation and 1977 Reorganization plans in the previous paragraph. At the time the People and Congress established the Department of Agriculture in the late 1800's, no one had any idea of where technology would be moving in one hundred years. This Office on the regulation of technology will be discussed at length below in the chapter on reassessing and restructuring public agencies. Grain inspections and stockyard administration are included in their own division established in 1994. The two major stated duties of this division as it was created were to guarantee a unified code to facilitate the duties of the inspectors, unions and for applying those Federal standards. The Packers and Stockyards Programs enforces the Packers and Stockyards Act of 1921. One of the alleged myths of the creation of this division was the packing and shipping of wormy and contaminated meat to the troops. This is discussed in depth below, however, it appears the citizens or the troops as they came marching home, began to realize they had a right to food that was of quality and safely processed and packed.

Food Safety and Food, Nutrition and Consumer Services also are separate divisions of the Department of Agriculture. Although related to the early founding reasons of the Department of Agriculture in the 1800's, food safety and consumer services by 1953 (5 U.S.C.app.) showed a demand by the citizens for better quality and humane treatment of their food resources. By 1981 the Reorganization Act Plan 2 (5. U.S.C. app 1981) was upgraded to fully serve the citizens of the United States of America to provide quality controls, standardizations, and high health and safety regulations and inspections to make sure the food we eat is healthful, nutritious, and safely grown, raised, slaughtered and packaged. In addition the Congress mandated the food, nutrition and consumer services to make sure people have food, and that all our nation's food is healthy and safe. The education of the public on nutrition and health is mandated to this division of the Department of Agriculture.

This area of the Department of Agriculture is of great importance as it is necessary in this current time of illegal smuggling of slaves to work on factory farms across the nation. The health and safety issues to the slaves create extreme danger to the nation from unsanitary and inhumane conditions of the workers. The arrest of July 24, 2017 in Florida of a big rig driver who left smuggled slaves in a big rig in the heat causing ten deaths (to date, others may die from the incident) leads us to wonder, if the citizen who heard a person begging for water and called police had not happened by, how many dead bodies would have just been buried in shallow graves in the fields where the slaves were to be taken to work.

Farm and Foreign Agricultural Services provides aid and loans to farmers to help stabilize our nation's food sources in spite of drought, flood, and other natural disasters. This division includes the Commodity Credit Corporation, a special program to stabilize, protect and support balanced commodity production, packaging, and consumer availability. Both Food Safety and the Farm services in these divisions are available to United States farming interests in foreign countries. This will be discussed at length below.

The Farm and Foreign Agricultural Services has a duty to assure the public that the food they are allowing into the country to keep the balance of food given out, or sold to balance needs and overages in other countries is properly inspected at all levels for health and safety of both workers and consumers. Eating food that is produced in fields or ponds where the local native populations or slave laborers go to the bathroom, bathe, and do laundry and dishes in the water then sprayed on the produce is NOT very appetizing and is in fact probably not healthy.

Research, Education, and Economics division of the Department of Agriculture
was established to advise, educate and promote the sustainable high quality safe food and
other agricultural resources to minimize the possibilities of famine, and/or starvation in
the United States of America. The President of the United States of America is given the
top priority duty of making sure there never is again a time when Americans suffer
starvation or inadequate nutrition. This will be discussed at length below as well.

The Natural Resources and Environment division of the Department of
Agriculture covers 75% of the land base of the United States of America. Without
adequate watershed, and wild lands, the geographic research has proven, agricultural
lands will falter, then fail. The dustbowls, floods, famines, and other natural disasters
have effect on the ability of the agricultural lands to produce adequate food and other
agricultural products to sustain the nation. It is the duty of this division to watch the
environment and nature itself to protect the agricultural balance for a sustained American
food source. This division includes the U S Forest service and the Farmland Preservation
Division. Support for all Department of Agriculture duties is given through the Graduate
School of the United States Department of Agriculture.

This last area is very important as we see a battle arising between foreign and
American mining interests and factory farm desire to put cattle on all the lands, thereby
disrupting the natural balance of wild animals, plants, and watersheds. In the past ten
years America has seen an dramatic increase in weather related damage to areas (Katrina,
while 12 years ago is a horrifying example of no one paying attention to the levee safety
and ability to do the job they were built to do to keep the waters from rushing over the
lands, whether cities or farmlands.

COMMERCE

The Department of Commerce and Labor was established by act of 1903 (15
U.S.C. 1501) and separated into The Department of Commerce by act 15 U.S.C. 1501 in

1913 the Department of Labor becoming a separate Department. The Department of Commerce encourages national and international trade, economic growth, and technological growth throw a variety of programs. The Department of Commerce offers assistance and information to free enterprise including education programs, research and support for national and international business programs. An important part of the Department of Commerce is to promote understanding and benefits of the commerce between businesses and governments. One area assigned to the Department of Commerce is the development of minority business and advisors, research and support for use of telecommunications, and technology for minority owned business.

The office of the Secretary is mandated to provide the President and Congress, and appropriate committees and councils with research, data, and advisory information on Commerce as well as people in business who request information and assistance in business questions to help improve commerce.

The Business Liaison office was established to provide the starting point for those who need information to be directed tot he appropriate resources for help.

BUREAU OF INDUSTRY AND SECURITY

Established in 1988 this Bureau was designed by Congress to advance U. S. national security, foreign policy and economic objectives by export controls, and policies and regulations (53 FR 20881). This Office controls and creates policies to protect legal exporters while controlling illegal exporters. This office of export enforcement also controls illegal technology transfers, and conducts cooperative enforcement activities for international trade.

Office of International Programs has a deceptively calm name, this office controls all aspects of export or trade of radiological weapons, nuclear, chemical, biological weaponry and the systems, commodities and technology and equipment to build these weapons of mass destruction. The systems and technology that are used to design or build such systems and technologies

Management and Policy Coordination unit establishes and evaluates the Bureau's overall policy agendas regarding provision of technical assistance for the ezport of weapons of mass destruction. This will be discussed at length in the following chapters.

ECONOMIC DEVELOPMENT ADMINISTRATION

Established in 1965 under The Public Works and Economic Development Act (42 U.S. C. 3121) as part of an effort to direct Federal assets to economically distressed areas. This Administration was mandated to assist rural and urban communities that were outside the mainstream economy and lagging in economic development.

ECONOMICS AND STATISTICS ADMINISTRATION

The economics and Statistics Administration provides broad and targeted economic, data, analyses and forecasts for use by domestic and international businesses, agencies and the general public.

The Census Bureau, and the Bureau for Economic Analysis are the responsibility of the Under Secretary while the Secretary is the advisor to the President on all matters within the jurisdiction of this Administration. The Bureau of Census was established by Act (32 Stat. 51) in 1902. The major functions are authorized by the Constitution which requires that a census be taken every ten years and codified under Title 13. The Census Bureau has expanded to include a variety of census reports to be used by government agencies and private businesses that need the types of information and statistics provided by the Bureau. These may include surveys on particular populations, particular numbers of employees in certain fields, trade and immigration census reports and advisories, publications of estimates and projections of the population based on census already taken and factors that restrict, or enhance economic, business, or population in certain geographic areas, and the nation as a whole. Today many of the reports and advisories are available free of charge on the Census official website, those requiring paper documents can be purchased them from the Bureau for a fee.

The Bureau of Economic Analysis promotes a better understanding to the public and to agencies requiring information, advisories and data in timely, accurate and cost effective means. Much of the data required is available free of charge from their web site.

The International Trade Administration was established in 1980 by the Secretary of Commerce to promote world trade and strengthen world trade and investment positions of the United States of America. Import Administration Office defends American industry against injurious and unfair trade practices. The anti-dumping and countervailing duty laws were put in place for this purpose and are administrated by this office. Market Access and Compliance office advises on the analysis, formulation and implementation of U S international business economic policies. This are will be discussed at length in a later chapter.

Manufacturing and Services Office of both foreign and domestic markets is an analysis and policy setting office of the International Trade Administration, the stated purpose in The Manual of The United States of America is to carry on programs of research and analysis of domestic and world markets to ensure that the American markets are not put in an injurious or unfair position in the global marketplace. This office will also be discussed at length in a later chapter.

The Manual of the United States Government contains a comprehensive list of the Export Assistance Centers maintained by the Department of Commerce International Trade Administration to help businesses in their knowledge of doing business with foreign countries.

The Minority Business Development Agency was established in 1969 by Executive Order. This Agency promotes and supports development and growth of small businesses owned and operated by minority persons (and women). The Agency was created to provide advice, support, and assistance to minority small businesses to overcome social and economic disadvantages that have created a limit on minority small business development in the past. There are three branches of this Agency:

Minority Business Opportunity committees which provide information, assistance and technological advisories on a web site and in programs offered from time to time.

The second promotes and coordinates the offerings of other Federal business agencies, councils and opportunities to keep minority business developers and owners aware of what help is available to them through the Federal government.

The agency directs Federal programs, through the activities of the agency, to facilitate information of opportunities for minority and women owned business being distributed to those to whom the Agency was created to assist.

NATIONAL OCEANIC AND ATMOSPHERIC ADMINISTRATION

The National Oceanic and Atmospheric Administration (NOAA) was formed in 1970 by the Reorganization Plan No. 4 (5 U.S.C.app.) The mission of NOAA is environmental assessment, prediction and stewardship. The monitoring and assessing of the state of the environment to protect life, property and natural resources and to promote economic well being of the United States. NOAA is also charged to enhance the environmental security of the United States, which will be discussed at length in later chapters. NOAA is the protector of Marine Resources including the ocean, coasts and living marine resources while promoting sustainable economic development. This aspect of NOAA will also be included in later chapters.

Other agencies included in NOOA are the National Weather Service, National Environmental Satellite and Data, and Information Service, National Marine Fisheries Service, National Ocean Service, Office of Oceanic and Atmospheric Research, and Office of Marine and Aviation Operations. Local offices of all these programs are listed in The Manual of The United States Government, updated annually. Much of the information from each office is available free on their web sites, or if needed in paper copy, can be obtained for a fee

THE NATIONAL TELECOMUNICATIONS & INFORMATIONADMINISTRATION

Established in 1978 by Reorganization Plan No. 1 of 1977 (5 U.S.C.app.) and Executive Order 12046 of 1978 (3 CFR, 1978 Comp. P. 158) by combining the offices of Telecommunications Executive Office of the President and The Department of Commerce Telecommunications offices into one agency. The new Office would report directly to the Secretary of Commerce. The functions of this Office are to create and maintain reports and policy mandates for the President as needed, to develop and present policies as the analysts and researchers recommend to the President, and to the Secretary of Commerce. To administrate grants, loans, and programs as directed by the President and Secretary of Commerce regarding telecommunications to the public, business, Congress, and Federal agencies as requested. To oversee the public transition to the digital network for telecommunications needs of the government and public.

The Office of Technology Policy provides policy makers with information and deeper understanding of technology as needed and requested. This Office also serves to be the ambassador of technology to industry to keep the businesses and industries up to date on how technology may help them increase their products, service and performance.

The National Institute of Standards and Technology operates under the National Institute of Standards and technology Act (15 U.S.C. 271) which amends the Organic Act of 1901 (ch.872 which created the National Bureau of Technology. The Office was renamed to National Institute of Standards and Technology in 1988 by Congress, which expanded the duties and mandates of the Institute. The Institute was given the duty to promote measurement science, standards, and technology to make production, standards, and improve the quality of life. This Office promotes high risk areas being resolved by scholarships, research grants, and promoting scientists to improve the technology for industry and government in areas of critical national need. This office will be discussed in later chapters.

The National Technical Information Service provides information to business, government and cities with the mandate to improve the quality of life. Much of the information is available on their web sites for free. Hard copy, or more extensive reports and research can be purchased for a fee.

United States Patent and Trademark Office

This office is the office established by Act of Congress (35 U.S.C. 1) 1952 that was expected to promote science and other useful arts by securing for limited timeframes to inventors the exclusive right to their respective discoveries. (Article1, Section 8 Constitution of the United States of America allows the registration of trademarks, as based on the Commerce Clause of the Constitution. This office will be discussed in later chapters.

DEFENSE

The Department of Defense is, as it is mandated, responsible for providing military forces needed to deter war, and to protect the security of our country. The President is the Commander in Chief, the Secretary of Defense is mandated to exercise authority, direction and control providing advice, command and direct the Joint Chiefs of Staff of the branches of the military and Guard.

The National Security Act amendments of 1949 re-designated the National Military Establishment as the Department of Defense and established it to the Executive Branch of government (10 U.S.C. 111). While headed by the Secretary of Defense, the President of the United States of America remains the Commander in Chief, and the person responsible for all acts of the Department of Defense. CONGRESS, in Article 1, section 8 of the Constitution is clearly the only branch of the government that can appropriate funds, levy taxes, or collect taxes for war. The National Security Act did not give the Department any more power than to be the military, there is no power for the

Department of Defense to do anything more than request funds in the prescribed manner, and allow Congress to decide whether or not to grant those funds.

As a further protection against the military trying to take over the country, the Constitution limits their funds and ability to act without a legislated act of war by Congress. However, the Constitution limits even Congress from appropriating money for any war for more than two years. This will all be discussed at length in later chapters. The Constitution notes that the President can veto any declaration of war, and the question must be returned to a full Congress for a new vote with two thirds of the vote of both houses being required to over rule the President's veto. This is further described according to the Rules and Limitations prescribed by the Case of a Bill rules and regulations for any Bill being disapproved by the President of the United States.

Office of the Secretary of Defense includes the offices of:

Acquisition, Technology and Logistics

The Under Secretary of Defense is responsible for the purchase of supplies, weaponry and all other purchases of the Department of Defense (DOD). This Office is responsible for the research and development of all supplies and weaponry that are used by the military. The Under Secretary reports to the Secretary and advises as requested to the President and Congress on the needs and costs of the military. Installation management, as well as technology development, engineering and testing and evaluation systems are all innovated by research and development programs through the office of the Under Secretary of Defense.

Networks and Information Integration

The Assistant Secretary of Defense is responsible through the office of Networks and Information Integration to take the materials and information from the office of the Under Secretary's division and ensuring superior support for missions, while exploiting or denying the enemy's ability to do the same. The Assistant Secretary of Defense gathers field information from the branches of the military, and advises the Secretary and the President on strategy and policy to successfully complete missions as assigned to the military by Congress and/or the President.

Personnel and Readiness

The Under Secretary of Personnel and Readiness has the duty to ensure at all times the United States military is prepared and ready to respond to any request of the Secretary of Defense as directed by the President and/or Congress. This office has the protocols and policies in place for immediate critical response for global response to situations in which the military is asked to respond. Training, Simulations developed and approved by the Under Secretary are utilized to keep the military in top conditioning for immediate response.

Policy

The Under Secretary of Defense for Policy is the lead staff advisor and assistant to the Secretary of defense on policy and protocol matters. The United States of America, through the Constitution has created safeguards to standing armies acting on their own. Strict policies and protocols are in place to ensure that the requirements of the Constitution are met. This position is of extreme importance because the approval of policy by the Under Secretary who is the main advisor to the Secretary of Defense, The President and Congress may either lead the United States to not properly protect America, or to allow America to become in violation of not only the Constitution, but of the United Nations and other world agreements regarding abuse of military power. This will be discussed in later chapters.

When considered how smoothly our military works, as seen in events such as 9/11 or in the daily performance of support services for troops, the Military which serves as many as 2 million enlisted personnel and a large number of civilian support personnel appears to be doing a good job meeting its mandates. While there are complaints, and scandals such as $900 toilet seats on ships in the Admiral's quarters, or $17 muffins at Defense Department meetings, the Department of Defense has a huge duty to protect Americans, and allied nations from the threat of war on our own lands. The Department of Defense, through the Joint Chief of Staffs, and the Secretary of Defense do have advisory jobs regarding warfare. However the Constitution has limited the declaration of War and financing of War to Congress.

JOINT CHIEFS OF STAFF

The Joint Chiefs of Staff consist of the Chairman, Vice Chair, the Chief of Staff of the Army, the Chief of Staff of the Navy, the Chief of Staff of the Air Force and the Commandant of the Marine Corps. The Chairman of the Joint Chiefs of Staff is the main advisor to the President, the National Security Council, and the Secretary of Defense. The complete honesty and adherence to the laws of the United States of America and the Global agreements for warfare rest on the shoulders of the Chairman of the Joint Chiefs of Staff for interpretation and network communication between the President and the military as well as Congress. The advice of the Chairman of the Joint Chiefs of Staff does not have to agree with that of the military Chiefs of Staff, nor the Generals in the field, nor the President or Congress, but as the policies are set and agreed upon the Chairman of the Joint Chiefs of Staff does have to respectfully adhere to the policies set by the President, the Secretary of Defense and Congress, and always must adhere to the Constitution of the United States of America and International law regarding warfare.

The Vice Chairman of the Joint Chiefs of Staff has the same duties and responsibilities as the Chairman, doing what is requested by the Chairman of the Joint Chiefs of Staff and trained to be at the ready should the Chairman of the Joint Chiefs of Staff not be able to perform the prescribed duties. The ongoing, seamless readiness and performance of the military is extremely important and can not be without specifically trained leadership. The Vice Chairman of the Joint Chiefs of Staff while serving holds the rank of general or admiral, and outranks every military leader except the Chairman of the Joint Chiefs of Staff.

JOINT STAFF

The Joint Staff is staff that works under the Joint Chief of Staff and the units necessary to complete the work of the Joint Chiefs of Staff. The Joint Staff is headed by a Director who is selected by the Chairman in consultation with the other Chiefs of Staff and approved by the Secretary of Defense. Officers selected to serve on the Joint Staff are selected in approximate equal numbers from the Army, Navy, Air Force and Marine Corps.

COMBATANT COMMANDS

The combatant commands are the commands that control and advise every area of actual active warfare and preparedness. The mission of combatant commands is to maintain the security and defense of the United States of America as directed from higher command. The Constitution of the United States, the Founders, and the Congress were concerned with wandering military going off on its own, and created through the years strict protocols to deter such actions. This area will be discussed in later chapters at length.

FIELD ACTIVITIES

The American Forces Information Service is responsible to prepare and disseminate information crucial to field operations. This information includes military command news resources, paper, internet, radio and field communications protocols and safety of communications technologies. The videos provided to all areas of the

Department of Justice regarding field activities are created and dispersed from the American Forces Information Service.

COUNTERINTELLIGENCE

The Counterintelligence Field activity was established in 2002 to build a Defense Counterintelligence System that would protect the joint forces and intelligence and critical assets from foreign intelligence, terrorists or other clandestine or covert threat. The Desired end stated in The Manual of The United States Government is a transformed Defense Counterintelligence system that synchronizes and integrate the Military Departments, the Joint Staff, Defense Agencies and Combatant Commands.

DEFENSE TECHNICAL INFORMATION CENTER

The Defense Technical Information Center is one of the offices that works under the auspices of the Under Secretary of Defense to provide defense scientific and technical information, and offer controlled information about the department of defense, designing and hosting more than 100 websites for the DOD. The material on these websites is day to day information, not classified or controlled materials.

DEFENSE TECHNOLOGICAL SECURITY ADMINISTRATION

The Defense Technological Security Administration is the office that creates, and supervises the development and implementation of technology. This office advises the Under Secretaries, the Secretary, the President and Congress, as well as the Joint Chiefs of Staff on technology as it relates to security and defense The Administration helps to build and implement the policies necessary to keep the United States military informed of the most modern technological advancements in order to know what other military might have access to, and be using, and how to keep a technological advantage.

EDUCATION

The Department of Defense since 1992 has maintained The Department of Defense Education Activity which operates the Department of Defense Dependents Schools and the Department of Defense Elementary and Secondary Schools for Military Dependents eligible for these education programs.

HUMAN RESOURCES AND MANPOWER

Established to meet the requirements of Congress in regards to the hiring, maintaining of staff, and benefits for DOD. This office handles areas of the military including Absentee ballot distribution and collection for stationed active duty personnel and civilian support employees, women's issues, the Sexual Assault Unit and language capabilities programs for the DOD.

HEALTH CARE

The TRICARE Management Activity was established in 1998 formerly known as CHAMPUS and the Defense Medical Programs Activity, as well as other health care programs formerly handled by the Assistant Secretary of Defense for Health Affairs. The mission is to manage the healthcare and manage and support health care for Uniformed Services in TRICARE and CHAMPUS as well.

TEST RESOURCE MANAGEMENT

This office works for the Under Secretary of Defense offices of Acquisition, Technology and Defense. The mission is to control and manage the test programs and to sustain approved services following testing in order to evaluate the product or service being tested. This office provides research and advisories on products and services to the Under Secretary which are utilized in reports, budgets, and evaluations to be available to the Secretary of Defense, the President, or Congress as requested. There are many levels of testing included in Test Resource Management, not just weaponry.

PRISONERS OF WAR AND MISSING PERSONNEL

This office was established in 1993 to manage prisoners of war, and missing United States Personnel and all the issues related to these circumstances. This Office creates policy advisories and carries out the directions of the Secretary of Defense in regards to prisoners of war and missing personnel, including periodic examination of documents that may determine the missing personnel has been located outside the military.

ECONOMIC ADJUSTMENT

This office assists communities adversely affected by closing of military bases or installations. This office operates through the Defense Economic Adjustment Program.

DEPARTMENT OF THE AIR FORCE

The Department of the Air Force, in its mission says, is responsible for defending the United States through control and exploitation of air and space. The United Nations, and many international air and space agreements are involved in the day to day work of the Air Force. The Air Force was established by the National Security Act of 1947 (61 Stat. 502). The National Security Act Amendments of 1949 redesignated the National Military Establishment as the Department of Defense and established it as an Executive Branch of the government. The Air Force was designated under the Department of Defense (63 Stat. 578), operating under the Secretary of Defense (10 U.S.C. 8010). The Department is led by the Secretary of the Air Force, the Air Staff and field Organizations Secretary

The Secretary of the Air Force is responsible for training, logistical support, maintenance, welfare of personnel, administration, recruiting, development and tasks assigned by the President of the United States or the Secretary of Defense.

Air Staff

The Air staff have the duty to provide professional assistance to the President or the Secretary of Defense and Joint Chiefs of Staff as required and requested.

Field Organizations

The Field Organizations are on a functional basis and responsible to provide the supplies, personnel, and weaponry with the support supplies, personnel and weaponry to accomplish requested and required tasks assigned by the DOD and The President and Joint Chiefs of Staff. The orders for the Field Organizations are approved by the Secretary of the Air Force before being implemented.

MAJOR AIR COMMANDS

The Major Air Commands make sure the directions and needs of the Field Organizations are ready and trained should they be required. When a command is given for active duty, the Major Air Commands are responsible for combat ready, rapid deployment in response to orders, whether for peacetime air sovereignty or wartime defensive actions. Each of the Commands below is expected to do what is required, keep at moment notice readiness for tactical alert, and to communicate upwards through the appropriate channels so the President, Congress and the Department of Defense, Chief of Staffs as well as the Air Force Commanders know the current status and needs of every Command.

AIR FORCE MATERIAL COMMAND

This command makes sure that the latest products, technology and materials are investigate and implemented if test proven to be able to advance the superiority of the

United States Air Force. This command makes sure all Air Force material, supplies, buildings and support services are at the ready for combat activation, should that be required. This Command oversees the single manager continuous product care and process improvement necessary to keep combat ready at all times.

AIR MOBILITY COMMAND

This command is the airlift support branch of the Air Force. Aero-medical evacuation response supplies, and equipment, air refueling and special air missions are continuously maintained for use upon request.

AIR FORCE RESERVE COMMAND

This command is the Reserve command and supports the Air Force mission of control and exploitation of air space. This is not a command held in reserve for crisis or war, it is a day by day command to support the Air Force.

AIR SPACE COMMAND

This command operates space and ballistic missile systems including warning systems of enemy ballistic missile systems, space, spacelift and satellite operations for the Air Force.

AIR SPECIAL OPERATIONS COMMAND

This command supports the special operations command. Deploying and delivering air support for special operations.

AIR EDUCATION AND TRAINING COMMAND

This command recruits, trains and provides education as needed for the various Air Force commands, including medical, readiness and security assistance areas of the Air Force.

OVERSEAS FIELD ACTIVITIES

AIR NATIONAL GUARD

The Air National Guard Center is responsible for operational and technical tasks to keep the Guard manned, equipped, and trained at readiness level at all times.

BASE CLOSURES

The Agency serves as the office responsible for disposal of property related to the 1988 and 1990 Base Closure and Realignment Acts.

COMMUNICATIONS

The Agency ensures that Air Force communication systems on the ground, in the air, domestic and foreign are up to date, and functioning properly at all times. The back up systems are also kept at the ready at all times by the communications Agency.

EMERGENCY PREPAREDNESS

National Security planning for any national emergency involving the Air Force is kept continually at the ready by this Agency. This office responsible to ensure there is a continuity of operations during any emergency.

ENGINEERING

Engineering is the Air Force Agency that provides support, maintenance advisory and training, vehicle and equipment research and development to ensure the Air Force is at the ready with the most current systems, vehicles, air and space equipment.

ENVIRONMENTAL QUALITY

This Agency ensures that the Air Force is in compliance with environmental rules, laws and regulations, as well as advising and implementing construction design and facilities design to be in compliance with environmental laws.

FLIGHT STANDARDS

The Flight Standards Agency is responsible for airfields, navigation systems, and instrument systems. This Agency inspects and ensures all of these are in continuously prepared status. Cockpit displays, air traffic control and airlift procedures as well as aero space management procedures are all standardized and the personnel and equipment are at emergency readiness at all times.

HISTORIC PUBLICATIONS

Historic publications researches, write, and preserves historical Air Force data, publications and other historical material for the use of headquarters as requested.

HISTORICAL RESEARCH

Historical Research keeps the material for historic publications and provides material and support to scholars and the general public about the Air Force.

INTELLIGENCE

The Intelligence Agency of the Air Force supports Air Force operations with data analysis and monitoring of weapons, space intelligence and information about weapons and products in use.

MEDICAL OPERATIONS

This Agency supports the Air Force Surgeon General in all aspects of plans, programs and policies for the Air Force missions and the personnel and their families. The monitoring and alerts for radiation as it pertains to the health of Air Force personnel and their families is included in this Agency.

MODELING AND SIMULATION

This Agency trains and plans, develops and implements modeling and simulation training for the Air Force.

NEWS

The Air Force maintains its own internal news systems. Paper, internet, radio and televised programming is the responsibility of the New Agency.

NUCLEAR WEAPON MONITORING

The Air Force maintains the compliance with nuclear treaties. This Agency follows and reports all nuclear testing both domestic and foreign to maintain treaties necessary for avoidance of nuclear war. This Agency conducts research and development as well as implementation of new systems that are better at detecting nuclear testing, and movement of nuclear material.

REAL ESTATE

This Agency manages, buys and disposes of land for the Air Force worldwide and maintains the immediate current status of all worldwide Air Force land and facilities.

WEATHER SERVICES

This Agency collects and disseminates the daily centralized weather support information necessary for the Air Force and the Army joint staff, designated commands . The Agency supports research and assessment of new technical systems to provide the most effective weather data possible to the Air Force.

DIRECT REPORTING UNITS include:

Air Force Communication and Information Center

This Center provides the information technology to other Air Force Centers and Agencies to improve operations and technological superiority to all areas of the Air Force.

Air Force Doctrine Center

This Center develops and publishes the doctrines for basic operational level doctrine for the Air Force. The Center ensures that the policies and doctrines of the Air Force are consistent with the other services and in compliance with all the policy laws and regulations of the United States. This Center does not address war activities, that work is done by another agency.

Air Force Security Forces Center

This Agency makes sure there is consistent Air Force Security for all areas the Air Force is globally.

Eleventh Wing

The Eleventh Wing supports Headquarters and other Air Force units in the National Capital Region. This is the agency that directs and deploys the Air Force Band, for ceremonies involving the White House, Arlington National Cemetery, The Air Force Chief of Staff and the Air Force Secretary.

United States Air Academy

Academic and military instruction is provided for Air Force students who may obtain a Bachelors Degree in Science

.

ARMY

The mission of the Army is to stay prepared to preserve the peace, security and the defense of our nation. The Army is specialized in land operations. The Army also responds to environmental programs to protect the environment, waterways, flood and beach erosion and water resource development. The Army provides military assistance to Federal, State and local government agencies including natural disaster assistance. THIS will be discussed in later chapters at length.

The Army was established by the Continental Congress on June 14, 1777. More than a year before the Declaration of Independence. The Department of War was established as an executive department ay Act approved August 7, 1789 (1 Stat. 49). The national Security act of 1947 established The Secretary of War at its head (4 U.S.C. 171) which was Amended in 1949 (63 Stat.578) which put the Department of the Army (formerly the Department of War as a military division of the Department of Defense.

ARMY STAFF

Army Staff is presided over by the Chief of Staff (Secretary of the Army). This division prepares for deployments, investigates and creates reports about all Army functions for a variety of reasons and annual reports, manages demobilizations.

PROGRAM AREAS

The program areas of the Army cover a vast number of duties for the Secretary, the Army Staff and the civil works duties of the Army.

CIVIL FUNCTIONS

These functions are the water resources, dams, waterways, ocean fronts, and many other engineering works, including disaster preparedness and response related to waterways of the United States of America, and as assigned by the Congress and/or President in crisis disasters concerning water. This office also handles bands, cemeteries, and all ceremonial staff and needs for the Army.

HISTORY

The historical office of the Army includes collection and archival services, public information services of historical resources for the Army, as well as advisory and historical services for ceremonies and historical property preservation for the Army.

INSTALLATIONS

This office manages the installations of the Army including all infrastructure, support and supplies for Army installations worldwide. Opening, closing, and maintaining bases, and family support, recreational support for the Army are included in the duties of keeping the installations crisis ready every moment.

INTELLIGENCE

The intelligence office is concerned with planning and managing Army Intelligence and staff. Threat models and simulators are included in the responsibilities of this office.

MEDICAL

This office plans, and implements personnel health services and management of health services for the Army, and other agencies and operations as requested. This office includes environmental programs and prevention of disease, as well as the budgeting, planning, programming for Army health services.

MILITARY OPERATIONS AND PLANS

This office implements planning from orders, can be civil, or Army orders. Law enforcement and crime prevention are included in this division.

RESERVE COMPONENTS

Army National Guard and U.S. Army Reserve units are coordinated through this office.

RELIGIOUS

Chapels, and Chaplains, liaison with civilian ecclesiastical agencies are all coordinated, trained, and overseen in this office for the Army.

UNITED STATES ARMY NORTH

A unique unit to provide homeland defense and support as well as civil support missions.

NAVY

The duty of the Navy is to protect the United States as Directed by The President, or the Secretary of Defense, at sea and with the Marine Corps the seizure or advanced set up of bases to support the Military of the United States, and at sea. This will be discussed at length in later chapters. The US Navy was founded in 1775 as the Continental Navy of the American Revolution. The Department of the Navy and the Secretary of the Navy were established by act on April 30, 1798 (10 U.S.C. 5011, 5031). The previous nine years the Department of War supervised the naval affairs under an Act of 1789 (1 Stat. 49). The National Security Act of 1949 established the Navy as a division of the United States Defense Department (63 Stat. 578). The Department of the Navy includes the Coast Guard and the United States Marine Corps.

SECRETARY

The Secretary of the Navy is appointed by the President and is under the United States Department of Defense Secretary. This administrative branch is called the executive administration of the Navy.

LEGAL

The Naval Judge Advocate branch is headed by a Judge Advocate General who provides all legal advice and related services for the Navy, except for advice provided by the General Counsel. The Legal division provides advice and support to the Secretary of the Navy in ethics, international law, Naval law, and technological and educational support through the Naval Justice School.

CRIMINAL INVESTIGATION

The Navy has its own criminal investigation teams, for ashore, or asea, these teams handle all criminal and counterintelligence work for the Navy, Marine Corps and Coast Guard.

RESEARCH

This division is in control of all research aspects of the Navy, Marine Corps and Coast Guard, including patents, research and copyrighting of Naval material initiated by the teams.

COMPUTERS AND TECHNOLOGY

This unit was formed in 2002 to merge space operations, satellite technology and all aspects of computer technology as it applies to the Navy.

EDUCATION AND TRAINING

This division in responsibility for Navy, Coast Guard, and some Marine Corps onshore training classes, material and system simulation training.

FACILITIES

The Naval Facilities unit handles all real estate, legal, and building plans, implementation and planning for all Naval Department real property, facilities and bases.

INTELLIGENCE

The Naval Intelligence division fulfills the requirements necessary for all Naval Intelligence projects, equipment and oversight.

MANPOWER

The Bureau of Naval Personnel directs the recruitment, transfer, direction for training, and benefits for the Department of the Navy.

MEDICINE

This department directs, and oversees medical and dental care for all personnel and their dependents. A major responsibility of this department is medical readiness preparedness for moment to moment readiness for war or natural disaster medical support for the Navy, Marine Corps and Coast Guard.

OCEANOGRAHPY

The science, engineering and technology for the Navy. This includes the ocean and the atmosphere and the effects on Naval operations moment to moment.

SEA SYSTEMS

This is the division that provides support to the Navy and upon request other military for sea travel, ships, subs, and sea platforms and seaboard combat weaponry and support technology, equipment and supplies.

SPACE AND NAVAL WARFARE

Technical and material support for any division of the Navy as requested and approved by the Department Secretary and the Secretary of Defense and President of the United States of America.

STRATEGIC SYSTEMS

Supplies the Navy, Marines, and Coast Guard with ballistic weapons materials and support. The specialized training and oversight of the personnel required for strategic systems security and safety.

SUPPLY SYSTEMS

This is the division that when requested obtains and transports supplies and maintains the war and disaster ready condition of all aspects of the Navy, Marine Corp and Coast Guard for immediate use as required by the Department of the Navy.

WARFARE DEVELOPMENT

This research and implementation division of the Navy interfaces with other Naval divisions to make sure the United States Navy, Marine Corps and Coast Guard are ready at all times for natural or manmade crisis as directed by the Secretary of the Navy.

UNITED STATES NAVAL ACADEMY

This four year undergraduate academy provides officer training as well as a well rounded basic four year college education to prepare young Naval, Marine, and Coast Guard personnel for officer level service to the United States.

INFORMATION SOURCES FOR THE PUBLIC

The Navy maintains information outreach for civilian recruiting to military positions, civilian support positions, as well as information regarding environmental studies, research, consumer reports, and general inquiries the public may have about the use of taxpayer funds for the Naval purposes.

MARINE CORPS

Established on November 10, 1775 by the Continental Congress before the Declaration of Independence and Constitution were formalized and instituted. Re-detailed in the Constitution (10 U.S.C. 5063). The Marine Corps is a Division of the United States Secretary of the Navy responsibilities.

DEFENSE AGENCIES

Defense Department has many other agencies within the Defense Department each having special duties but must be overseen by the appropriate Defense Secretary office or under secretary.

DEFENSE ADVANCED RESEARCH PROJECT AGENCY

Under the direction and authority of the under secretary of defense, this agency is responsible for research and development of advanced systems projects as requested by the military and the President, Secretary of Defense. The job of this agency is to plan and implement what is needed to create what the military needs to stay prepared for advanced warfare technology and skills.

DEFENSE BUSINESS TRANSFORMATION AGENCY

Established in 2005, this agency was created to improve the DOD business operations.

DEFENSE COMMISARY AGENCY

Established in 1990 this office oversees the commissary supplies and needs for the military forces worldwide overseen by the Secretary of Defense.

DEFENSE CONTRACT AUDIT AGENCY

This office has five main offices and 70 regional offices that manage the audits on the Defense contracts. The offices are in the United States and overseas. The General Accounting Office has a duty to oversee any government spending and report to Congress and the President. Vice President Al Gore was working on EBT programs to make sure where every penny of taxpayer money was going and accounted for. This will be discussed at length in later chapters.

DEFENSE CONTRACT MANAGEMENT AGENCY

This office was established by the Deputy Secretary of Defense in 2000. This is a significant date, a fuller discussion will be in later chapters. This agency manages acquisitions under the office of the Under Secretary of Defense Acquisitions, Logistics and Technology Office.

DEFENSE FINANCE AND ACCOUNTING SERVICE

Established in 1991 this office works with the Under Secretary of Defense, Comptroller Chief Financial Officer to strengthen and reduce costs for the military. This office researches prepares, and keeps business intelligence and management reports available to the Department of Defense and the President.

DEFENSE INFORMATION SYSTEMS AGENCY

Established in 1960 as the Defense Communications Agency, the Defense Information Systems Agency is under the Assistant Under Secretary of Defense. This Agency plans, develops, supports, does field operations, support commands, controls communication and information systems for the President, Vice President, Secretary of Defense, Joint Chiefs of Staff and the combat commanders during peace and war,

DEFENSE INTELLIGENCE AGENCY

The Defense Intelligence Agency was established in 1961 and operates under the control and direction of the Under Secretary of Defense for intelligence regarding the military. The mission of this Agency is to provide intelligence to all branches of the military, the President, and Vice President and Secretary of Defense in peacetime or war processing and passing on intelligence from other areas of the Government.

DEFENSE LEGAL SERVICES AGENCY

The Defense Legal Service agency was established in 1981 under the direction, and control, and authority of the general Counsel of the Department of Defense and its Director. This Agency provides legal support and legislative advice on Presidential Executive Orders and provides the central documentation for Congress reference and distribution within the Department of Defense. The Legal Services Agency also keeps the historical legislative files and administers programs for alternate dispute resolution within the Defense Department.

DEFENSE LOGISTICS AGENCY

The Defense Logistics Agency is under the authority of the Under Secretary for Logistics for Acquisition, Technology and Logistics, this office supports acquisition and needs for weapon acquisition and logistics for the military and a number of other Federal agencies but are limited to eight major commodities: fuel, food, clothing, construction materials, general supplies, electric supplies, and industrial and medical supplies.

DEFENSE SECURITY COOPERATION AGENCY

The Defense Security Cooperation Agency was established in 1971 and is under authority of the Under Secretary of Defense for Policy. This Agency executes the traditional security assistance as required by international military education and training and foreign military sales, program management for humanitarian assistance, demining and other DOD programs as requested by the Under Secretary.

DEFENSE SECURITY SERVICE

The Defense Security Service is under authority of the Under Secretary of Defense for Intelligence and ensures the safeguarding of classified information used by contractors on behalf of the Department of Defense and 22 other agencies in the Executive Branch. This agency is responsible for counterintelligence missions to integrate counterintelligence principle into security counterintelligence missions and to support the national counterintelligence strategy.

DEFENSE THREAT REDUCTION AGENCY

Established in 1998 this Agency is through the office of the Under Secretary of Defense-acquisitions division. The mission is to reduce the threat of weapons of mass destruction. This office implements weapons control treaties, and operates both offensive and defensive technology and operational concepts.

MISSILE DEFENSE AGENCY

This agency establishes, controls and deploys defensive missile systems. This office operates under the control of the Undersecretary of Defense for acquisitions.

NATIONAL GEOSPATIAL –INTELLIGENCE AGENCY

Established in 1996, this agency is under the authority of the Under Secretary of Defense Intelligence. This agency works continually to analyze and utilize intelligence from geospatial resources to support our National Security and the ability of combat units.

NATIONAL SECURITY AGENCY/CENTRAL SECURITY SERVICE

The NSA was established formally in 1952, and the Central Security Service was added in 1972 as departments of the Under Secretary of Intelligence. Signals, systems, and intelligence analysis are included in the duties of both NSA and CSS.

PENTAGON FORCES PROTECTION AGENCY

Established in 2002 as part of the National response to 9/11 this agency was designed to protect the Pentagon and DOD workforce and facilites under the authority of the Director of Administration and Management in the Office of the Secretary of Defense.

JOINT SERVICES SCHOOLS

There are several services schools that were created to meet the demands for specialized training and technology for specific Department of Defense employees. The employees and trainees may be military, or civilian support for military. These schools prepare the curriculum and make sure every graduate meets the standards of the positions to ensure our nation's security.

JOINT MILITARY INTELLIGENCE COLLEGE

Established in 1962 this college works under the direction of the Department of Defense Intelligence Agency Director. This specialized school is for educating all branches of the military intelligence personnel as they are required by their job descriptions. This college offers a Bachelor of Science in Strategic Intelligence to pre-approved students for the Department of Defense.

NATIONAL DEFENSE UNIVERSITY

Established in 1976 this University several colleges and college level programs as required for Department of Defense positions. Civilians in positions that require this specialized education are eligible to attend, as well as military personnel who require specialized training to continue or advance their careers.

NATIONAL WAR COLLEGE

Established to educate military and civilian personnel on National Security policy and implementation, this college is limited to specified career military and outside civilian support personnel for the programs required by their positions.

INDUSTRIAL COLLEGE OF THE ARMED FORCES

This college also is open to military and civilian support personnel who require specialized education for their positions. The Industrial College includes in its curriculum military leadership in security area positions This college is a two semester, rigorous program for those with Bachelors Degrees, who will, upon successful completion be awarded a Masters Degree   in National Resource Strategy.

JOINT FORCED STAFF COLLEGE

An intermediate and senior level joint college in the professional military educational systems, This school is dedicated to the skills of working together in the joint staff positions and the joint military operations going on daily around the world. There are several schools included in the college, Joint Advanced Warfighters School, Joint and Combined Warfighters School, Joint Continuing and Distance Education School, and the Joint Command, Control and Information Operations School.

INFORMATION RESOURCES MANAGEMENT COLLEGE

Graduate level courses in information management are offered in this college to promote the management level information resource programs having curriculum training for their own specialties. Many areas are covered: policy, strategic planning, leadership, management, process improvement, capital planning and investment, performance and results based management, technology assessment, architecture, information assurance, and security, acquisition, domestic preparedness transformation, e-Government, and information systems.

UNIFORMED SERVICES UNIVERSITY OF THE HEALTH SCIENCES

Established by Act in 1972 (10 U.S.C. 2112) the Uniformed Services University of Health Services was created to educate career oriented medical staff officers for the Military and Public Health Services. The students are primarily selected from military candidates, and must pass a process and appraisal of personal characteristics by the Board of Regents. All students become commissioned officers of the branch of the military they will be serving, or as assigned by the Board of Regents if assigned to a joint, or public health or Veterans Administration position.

THE DEPARTMENT OF EDUCATION

The Department of Education establishes policy and administrates and coordinates most Federal Assistance for Education in America. The mission is to ensure equal access to education and to promote educational excellence throughout the nation.

SECRETARY OF EDUCATION

The Secretary of Education is appointed by and advises the President of the United States of America under the Department of Education Act (20 U.S.C. 3411). The

Secretary is given the duty of ensuring the mission is implemented with equality and excellence across the nation.

ACTIVITIES

INSTITUTE OF EDUCATION SCIENCES

Institute of Education Sciences was formally established by the Education Sciences Reform Act of 2002 to focus on research, special education research, statistics and to support research activities needed to improve education policy and practice.

ELEMENTARY AND SECONDARY EDUCATION

This office directs policy for national elementary and secondary Education. Grants and contracts to the States are controlled from this office. This office directs policy for K-12, although in recent years most States and the Office have included pre-kindergarten education readiness programs as well. Special Education is included as well.

ENGLISH LANGUAGE ACQUISITION

The Office of English Language Acquisition and English Language Enhancement and Academic Achievement for students with a primary home language other than English is expected to set Federal Standards on language proficiency and excellence standards for students to be able to achieve all standards of American school children.

FEDERAL STUDENT AID

Title IV Higher Education Act of 1965 provisions are managed by the Federal Student Aid Office to provide access to a greater number of American post secondary students who qualify for the programs. The office implements and oversees all contracts for Federal Student Aid.

INNOVATION AND IMPROVEMENT

The office of Innovation and Improvement oversees grants for improving schools, includes special education and Family Policy Compliance Grants and implementation of new programs.

POSTSECONDARY EDUCATION

The Office of Postsecondary Education establishes policy, and oversees post secondary education, both standards and needs across the nation. The mission is to increase access to quality postsecondary education. One stated goal is to provide better access to teacher education in order to have more quality education for the nation's children and secondary education programs.

SPECIAL EDUCATION AND REHABILITATIVE SERVICES

This office charged with the duty to ensure that leadership and resources are provided to ensure people with disabilities have an equal opportunity to lean, work and live as fully integrated members of society. Special Education, Early Childhood Programs to help all children be able to successfully get an education, and Rehabilitation programs to support rehabilitation and independent living for disabled children and teens as they grow in to adulthood are all authorized in this Office.

VOCATIONAL AND ADULT EDUCATION

Administrates grants, contacts and technical assistance for vocational and technical education for adult education and literacy program.

FEDERALLY AIDED CORPORATIONS

These corporations, mostly non-profit corporations have been established to help specific members of society to gain equality through special education and programs to assist their ability to live and function as independently as possible in our society.

AMERICAN PRINTING HOUSE FOR THE BLIND

Established in 1858 as a non-profit organization, the American Printing House for the Blind received a Federal Charter in 1879 by the Act to promote Education of the Blind. This Act designates APHB as the primary and official supplier of education materials adapted for students who are legally blind and enrolled in formal educational programs below college level. Today this includes large type books, and equipment, Braille typewriters, and computerized programs and hardware to facilitate their learning process. The program materials are provided as allotments to the States as required.

GALLAUDET UNIVERSITY

Established in 1864, Gallaudet University is currently authorized under the Deaf Act of 1986, Gallaudet is a private, non-profit educational institution providing elementary, secondary undergraduate and continuing education programs for the deaf. This is an institute accredited by several accrediting agencies.

LAURENT CLERC NATIONAL DEAF EDUCATION CENTER

This Center is operated under authorization of the 1986 Education of the Deaf Act (20. U.S.C. 4304, as amended). The primary purpose is to develop and implement strategies for the deaf student in a variety of educational settings. Included in the work done by this Center is the development of non-English speaking deaf students to the programs available to them.

MODEL SECONDARY SCHOOL FOR THE DEAF

Established by Act of October, 1966 (20 U.S.C. 693) This model secondary school for the deaf has been superceded by Act as amended in 1986. The model school provides day and residential programs to deaf students from across the nation.

KENDALL DEMONSTRATION ELEMENATARY SCHOOL

The Nations first demonstration elementary school for the deaf was established by Act of December 1970 (20 U.S.C. 693) This Act was superceded by the Education of the Deaf Act of 1986 as amended. This school is for deaf students, a day school for onset of deafness to grade 8 in the Washington DC area.

HOWARD UNIVERSITY

Established by Act in 1867 (14 Stat. 438), Howard offers instruction in 12 schools and colleges. These are: arts and sciences, dentistry, engineering, architecture and computer sciences, medicine, pharmacy, nursing and allied health sciences, the graduate school, communications, divinity, education, law and social work. Also offered are special programs on cancer, child development, computational science and engineering, international affairs, sickle cell disease and national human genome project.

NATIONAL INSTITUTE FOR LITERACY

The NIL provides leadership for literacy issues, including improvement of reading instruction for children, youth, and adults . This Institute serves as the national resource on current and comprehensive literacy research, practice and policy.

NATIONAL TECHNICAL INSTITUTE FOR THE DEAF/ ROCHESTER INSTITTUTE OF TECHNOLOGY

Established by Act of Education for the Deaf in 1965 (20 U.S.C. 681) this Institutes was created to improve and promote education and employment of deaf persons in technical and engineering areas. The Act was superseded by the Deaf Education Act of 1986 (20 U.S.C. 4431, as amended) and continues its work currently.

ENERGY

The Department of Energy's mission is to foster a secure and reliable energy system. One that is economically and economically sustainable. To steward the nuclear weapons and to clean up the Departments facilities are the duties of this department, as well as to advance the science and National research systems for the energy Department divisions.

The Department of Energy Act of 1977 (42 U.S.C. 7131) consolidated the major Federal energy functions into one Cabinet level Department.

SECRETARY

The Secretary of Energy decides policy for Federal, State and local energy related matters, as well as is the chief advisor to the President on Energy.

INTELLIGENCE AND COUNTERINTELLIGENCE

The office of Intelligence and Counterintelligence ensures that all the departmental intelligence information requirements are met, and distributed to the appropriate officers in the Department and to the Secretary. This office ensures effective use of the US Governments intelligence apparatus in support of the needs of the Department of Energy's need for domestic and foreign threats and natural situations.

THE OFFICE OF HEALTH, SAFETY AND SECURITY

This Office ensures the health, safety and security policies to facilitate the Department of energy to protect national security and critical assets entrusted to the Department of Energy.

ENERGY PROGRAMS

Renewable energy. This Office is responsible to develop and support research in renewable and sustainable energy systems and production. Another function of this Office is to maintain ongoing development and implementation of energy saving programs for all government involved programs, including transportation, building use, industrial uses of energy programs from Federal, State to local. In addition, this Department of Energy Office is responsible to develop, and create financing for weatherization and protection of the poor, and disadvantaged. All government buildings, Federal, State and local can utilize this Office with research, and policy to develop and implement energy efficiency in construction and operation of government buildings.

FOSSIL ENERGY

This Research Lab project is supposed to keep current on all aspects of oil, gas, and fossil energy use and resource collection to facilitate the safety and capabilities of the nation to meet energy needs working with the private sector. This Office manages the Northeast Reserve, the naval petroleum shale reserve, and the strategic national reserve.

NUCLEAR ENERGY

This Office manages the research and development projects related to nuclear energy associated with fission and fusion energy. This applies to Naval and civilian nuclear reactor development, nuclear fuel cycles, and space nuclear applications. This office oversees particular kinds of fusion and fission products that are sold to foreign governments for medical use only. This office oversees and conducts technical analyses concerning nonproliferation, assesses alternative nuclear systems and reactor and fuel cycle concepts, manages hexafluoride activities and highly enriched uranium downblends, natural uranium sales and enrichment legacy activities. This office also evaluate proposed advanced nuclear fission energy concepts and technical improvements for powerplant possible applications.

ENERGY INFORMATION

This office administrates the information available to government and non-government sources of energy data collected, categorized, and maintained by the Department of Energy.

ELECTRICITY DELIVERY AND ENERGY RELIABILTY

This Office is expected to modernize and expand the electricity capabilities of the United States. Security and reliability of the energy infrastructure and facilitates the recovery from disruptions to the system.

NUCLEAR SECURITY PROGRAMS

Created by Act (113 Stat.512) in 2000, the Nuclear Security Systems Administration to focus the management of defense and security systems. The four offices listed above were reconstituted under one office of the Department of Energy

DEFENSE ACTIVITIES

This Office is responsible to oversee all nuclear branches within the United States for defense, anti-terrorism surveillance, and other duties as assigned by the Secretary of Defense.

NAVAL REACTORS

This Office manages and oversees the Naval Reactors including maintenance, development of new technology, implementation of new technology and programs.

NUCLEAR NONPROLIFERATION

This Office oversees and develops as well as implements programs, policy, procedures and research and development dealing with non –proliferations, control of exports and moving of fissile materials.

ENVIRONMENTAL QUALITY PROGRAMS

This office, established by the Nuclear Waste Policy Act of 1982 (42 U.S.C. 10101, et seq) as amended provides for the permanent, safe, geographic disposal of spent nuclear fuel and high level radioactive waste.

ENVIRONMENTAL MANAGEMENT

This office of the Assistant Secretary for Environmental Management is to manage safe cleanup and closure of sites, and facilities, waste management for nuclear waste, and provides innovative research and implementation programs to ensure safe and environmentally secure nuclear waste management.

LEGACY MANAGEMENT

This Office has the sole responsibility to track and ensure the continued safe and environmental storage and waste management of nuclear waste.

SCIENCE PROGRAM OFFICE

This Office has the mission to encourage ongoing research in all areas of the management and handling of nuclear energy and waste. These State of the Art facilities are open to scientists, both public, educational, and private company system backed to ask questions, pose research issues, and to come to find advice for situations that arise, either in the development, use, or waste management of nuclear fissile products and services.

FEDERAL ENERGY REGULATORY COMMISSION

An Independent Agency within the Department of Energy which regulates interstate transmission of electricity, natural gas, and oil.

POWER ADMINISTRATIONS

Administrates the Federal Hydroelectric plants and four Power Administrations

OPERATIONS AND FIELD OFFICES

These Operations and Field Office facilities are operated by contract for the management of the four area Administration offices.

BONNEVILLE/SOUTHERASTERN/ WEST and SOUTHWESTERN POWER ADMINISTRATIONS

Each of these four Federal Energy programs is under the authority of the Federal Energy Regulatory Commission Power Administrators to operate the facilities and utilize other offices and science services to keep all the areas operating safely and with efficient, technology as science becomes more energy knowledgeable.

HEALTH AND HUMAN SERVICES

The mission of the Department of Health and Human Services encompasses more humans than any other personal service aspect for those the enabling legislation required to be covered in the work for the residents of the United States of America. From pre-birth to the elderly, Health and Human Services was created by Act in 1953 (5 U.S.D. app.). Originally named The Department of Health Education and Welfare.

SECRETARY

The Secretary of HHS is the direct advisor to the President of the United States of America regarding health, housing, and welfare of the public. This Department was to address the enabling legislation mandate that the President of the United States of America has the duty to see that NO person on the lands of the United States, or its territories be impoverished, or suffer the effects of impoverishment (THE MANUAL OF THE UNITED STATES GOVERNMENT, 2004). This was removed from the 2008 Manual, however, this will be discussed in later chapters.

ADMINISTRATION ON AGING

This Administration has the duty to ensure that the aging are helped to maintain independence and dignity in their homes and communities. This Administration develops policies, plans and programs to ensure these mandated goals.

ADMINISTRATION ON CHILDREN AND FAMILIES

This Office provides advice to the secretary on policy, plans and programs for children on the soils of the United States of America and its territories and occupied lands. In 2008 the manual had been changed to say legal immigrants. This will be discussed in later chapters.

AGENCY FOR HEALTHCARE RESEARCH AND CONTROL

This Agency is charged with improving the safety, quality and availability of medicine in America.

AGENCY FOR TOXIC SUBSTANCES AND DISEASE REGISTRY

This Agency is charged with the oversight of all toxic substances and the disease registry to increase prevention and preparation for accidental toxic or disease situations from the environment.

CENTERS FOR DISEASE CONTROL AND PREVENTION

The Centers for Disease Control and Prevention are charged with providing leadership and direction in public health emergencies, and oversight of public health crisis.

MEDICARE AND MEDICAID SERVICES

Formerly known as the Healthcare Financing Administration this agency was created to administrate all Federal medical programs.

FOOD AND DRUG ADMINISTRATION

Charged with protecting the public health by ensuring the safety of foods and drugs used by humans and by veterinarians for animals. Cosmetics, radiation related health products and services, medical devices and biological products are included in the products administrated by this agency.

HEALTH RESOURCES AND SERVICES ADMINISTRATION

Charged with improving access to health care services for people who are uninsured, isolated or medically vulnerable. Oversees the tissue and organ transplant systems for the nation, as well as the vaccine injury compensation and reporting programs.

INDIAN HEALTH SERVICES

This agency is supposed to coordinate Federal, State, local and Native Nations programs to ensure healthcare services to the Nations Native Americans.

NATIONAL INSTITUTES OF HEALTH

The National Institutes support research and supports biomedical and behavioral research domestically and abroad. This Institute conducts research in its own labs as well as oversees research and development in public and private research programs.

SUBSTANCE ABUSE AND MENTAL HEALTH SERVICES ADMNISTRATIONS

This Agency funds, and oversees programs that research and treat persons with substance abuse, and mental health problems. The mission of this agency is to improve the quality, availability and range of substance abuse and mental health programs across the nation.

HOMELAND SECURITY

The Department of Homeland Security was established by the Homeland Security At of 2002 (6 U.S.C. 101 note) and came into implementation January 24, 2003. Administrated through the Secretary of Homeland Security.

HOUSING AND URBAN DEVELOPMENT

The Department was established by the Housing and Urban Development Act (42 U.S.C. 3532-3537). Created to administer principle programs that provide assistance for housing and the development of the Nation's communities. The program areas include the divisions of Fair Housing, Community Planning and Development, Fair Housing and Equal Opportunity, Federal Housing Enterprise Oversight for Fannie Mae and Freddie Mae Federal Housing mortgage programs. The government National Mortgage Association is a division known as Ginnie Mae to support FHA and VA mortgage loan programs. Additional areas are Housing, Healthy Homes and Lead Hazard Control, Public and Native American Housing Programs are also included in the HUD programs and plans.

INTERIOR

The Department of the Interior is to protect and provide access to the Nation's national natural and cultural heritage, and honor our trust responsibilities with the Native Nations and our commitments to island communities. Created by Act in 1849 (43 U.S.C. 1451) and reorganized in the Reorganization Plan No 3 of 1950 as amended (5 U.S. C. app.) The Department of the Interior is the Direct advisor to the President on all operations assigned to the Department by Act of Congress.

The divisions of the Department of the Interior are: Fish, Wildlife and Parks, Land and Minerals management, Indian (Native American) Affairs and Insular Affairs for the territory islands: American Samoa, Guam, the US. Virgin Islands, and the Commonwealth of the Northern Mariana Islands in developing effective government by providing financial and technical assistance. The Federated States of Micronesia, the Republic of the Marshall Islands,and the Republic of Plau, te Palmyta Atoll excluded areas and the Midway Atolls non-terrestrial areas are also under the authorization of the Department of the Interior.

JUSTICE

The Department of Justice represents the citizens as counsel for the citizens. It represents them in enforcing the law in the public interest. The main duty is to protect the citizens from criminals and subversion, ensuring healthy business competition, safeguarding the consumer and enforcing drug, immigration and naturalization laws. Established June 1870 by Act (28 U.S.C. 501,503, 509 note) the Department is supervised with the Attorney General of The United States of America as its head counsel and to advise the President on issues of justice pertaining to the nation.

ATTORNEY GENERAL

The Attorney General represents the United States of America inlegal manuals in general, and gives advice and opinions to the President and Executive Office Secretaries and Division Directors as requested. In cases of exceptional gravity to the United States the Attorney General appears in person to the Supreme Court of the United States.

COMMUNITY RELATIONS SERVICE

This office offers assistance to communities in resolving disputes related to race, color or national origins. The office also offers facilitation on development of alternates to coercion, violence, or litigation. This office also supports communities I development and implementation of local proactive measures to prevent or reduce racial/ethnic tensions.

PARDON ATTORNEY

The Pardon Attorney investigates cases and makes recommendations to the President involving Presidential Pardons. This office prepares the final report on the investigations that will go to the President following requests.

SOLICITOR GENERAL

This office represents the United States Government in cases involving the Supreme Court. Preparation of cases, and the decisions of whether the United States will appeal lower Court judgments against the government, or let them sit.

U.S. TRUSTEES PROGRAM

Established by The Bankruptcy Reform Act 1978 (11 U.S.C. 10 et seq) this program was established to protect the integrity of the bankruptcy system from fraud and abuse. This program operates in all States except Alabama and North Carolina. The Bankruptcy Abuse Prevention and Consumer Protection Act of 2005 (11 U.S.C. 101 note) significantly expanded the Program to prevent Fraud and Abuse. This office provides the day-to-day policy and legal direction, coordination and control for Bankruptcy.

DIVISIONS

ANTITRUST DIVISION

This office operates to support and prosecute the nations anti-trust laws to keep the market open and competitive. This involves reviewing proposed mergers, This office can charge both fines and criminal prosecutions and prison time for serious violations of the nations anti-trust laws. The venue of this division is national as well as international in scope. The antitrust Division also provides advice to other government agencies regarding anti-trust laws and applications.

CIVIL DIVISION

The Civil Division of the Department of Justice handles many types of cases involving the Federal Government, President, and agencies of the Federal government. The agency also advises on civil issues to appropriate Federal government agencies and cases. The cases may be filed by constituents, or be in support of consumers in large health and safety or consumer rights cases.

CIVIL RIGHTS DIVISION

This Division handles cases involving the Federal Government and civil rights claims, as well as watch dogging various agencies, and large consumer companies for abuses of the civil rights laws. This office was established in 1957 to ensure Civil Rights at the Federal level.

CRIMINAL DIVISION

The Criminal Division prosecutes and defends criminal cases involving the Federal Government. The cases vary in case content from violations of Federal law that are serious enough to be considered criminal, or are criminal in the Acts or amending statutes that create the Federal law in question.

ENVIRONMENTAL AND NATURAL RESOURCES DIVISION

This Division is charged with protecting the public, public lands and enforcing environment and land protection Acts and laws being adhered to.

NATIONAL SECURITY DIVISION

This Division is involved primarily with antiterrorism and anti espionage cases and is designed to support the laws legislated to protect the United States in these areas. This division is also responsible for all agencies adhering to the laws of implementation and practice of espionage, and anti-terrorism.

TAX DIVISION

This Division was established to provide the prosecutions and advisories in all tax areas for the Federal Government and some State Courts as detailed in the legislation.

BUREAUS

THE FEDERAL BUREA OF INVESTIGATION

This is the principle investigative arm of the Department of Justice. Like the above listed divisions, the Bureau has a variety of cases and rights to investigate to provide the supportive material to the Department of Justice and to the division appropriate to follow through on the information filed to be evaluated for prosecution, or not.

An important note, July 26, 2017, the current problems with the FBI and the political climate make reading all the material IN the Manual of The United States Government as well as supportive and definitive material critical for every voter. The FBI is as stated ONLY the investigative arm of the Department of Justice. As can be read in the Manual of The United States Government, the FBI is NOT a separate part of government and has NO power on its own.

This would make most of the rhetoric of the past year or more regarding the FBI moot. The Manual clearly states the FBI has a variety of cases and rights to investigate to provide SUPPORTIVE material to the Department of Justice and to the division appropriate to FOLLOW THROUGH on the information filed to be evaluated for prosecution or NOT.

The Department of Justice therefore has the DUTY to act on the information and to ask for supportive information or further investigation of matters as requested by THE DEPARTMENT OF JUSTICE, not by anyone at whimsy in the government.

The three main branches of government Executive, Legislative and the Supreme Court are given the RIGHT to ask for information, however, the CONGRESS for the most part is NOT the appropriate Constitutional branch of government to decide about prosecutions of cases or NOT. Only in cases of impeachment are the Senate and House given ANY right to prosecute, or hear cases, ALL other cases must be heard under the appropriate courts as indicated by the CONSTITUTION itself. While thousands of regulations and rules have been added over the two centuries since the Constitution was written, those rules and regulations are ALL under DUTY to be Constitutional as to what cases can be heard or investigated by which branches of government.

When the PEOPLE know the law, they are less likely to be stooges at the mercy (which there is none) of those who twist the truth for their own benefit.

BUREAU OF PRISONS

The Bureau of Prisons mission is established to protect the citizens from a variety of Federal criminals. The mission also includes the admonition to provide the confinement in a humane system that provides work and rehabilitation for the criminals. Included in this Bureau is the Correctional Programs Division, which includes education, religious and self-improvement opportunities for prisoners to become law abiding citizens. Other divisions of the bureau are the witness protection programs and community confinement agreements and implementations for non-violent criminals who are given out of prison paroles that contain community self-improvement contracts.

The Mandates of the legislations that formed the Bureau of Prisons are clear. There is not one word that describes the inhumane, over crowded warehouses that are often the reality of prisons. The Constitution gives the Bureau of Prisons the DUTY to make sure that EVERY prisoner is given the EQUAL treatment of any other prisoner. Every citizen needs to be aware of the legislation and mandates for the Bureau of Prisons and how they are doing their job.

The mandate to provide work and rehabilitation for the criminals is interesting in the supportive studies and material that prove that putting criminals in a relatively small space without proper programming to help them be rehabilitated and have something better to do with their time in incarceration than learning how to be better criminals and hate the society that sent them to be given NO assistance to examine and rebuild their lives and become better, safer citizens. The lack of oversight to make sure that prisoners are either given the benefits of the legislated rights in prison creates the reality of our prison system today.

UNITED STATES MARSHALS SERVICE

The United States Marshals Office is the nation's oldest law enforcement agency. The Marshalls Office was established in 1789 and serves as a vital link between the three branches of government. The Agency performs a number of duties, including: support and protection for Federal Courts, as well as jurors and participants in the trials and hearings; apprehending Federal fugitives and executing Federal warrants;

INTERNATIONAL CRIMINAL POLICE ORGANIZATION-UNITED STATES NATIONAL CENTRAL BUREAU

This is the United States office of law enforcement that interacts with INTERPOL. This office is the liaison for all aspects of international criminal police work.

DRUG ENFORCEMENT ADMINISTRATION

Created July 1973 by the Reorganization Plan No. 2 of 1973 (4 U.S.C.app.) the DEA enforced narcotics and controlled substance laws for the United States of America as well as Federal money laundering and bulk currency smuggling when the sales involve narcotics or controlled substances.

OFFICES OF JUSTICE PROGRAMS

Established by the Justice Assistance Act of 1984 these offices serve a variety of programs including: Assistance and programs to States to combat violent crime; The Bureau of National Crime Statistics; National Institute of Justice for research and development of justice programs; Juvenile Justice and Delinquency Prevention Programs; the Office for Victims of Crimes; the Drug Court Office for Improving and implementing new drug prevention programs; The Correction Programs Office; the Executive Office for Weed and Seed; The Office for Domestic Preparedness Support to develop and implement programs domestic safety against terrorism in the country; The Office of Police Corps and Law Enforcement Education provides college educational assistance to students who commit to public service.

OFFICE ON VIOLENCE AGAINST WOMEN

Established in 2005 this Office researches, develops and implements programs to prevent domestic violence and crimes against women and girls

BUREAU OF ALCOHOL, TOBACCO, FIREARMS AND EXPLOSIVES

Established by Department of Treasury Order No. 221 this bureau from IRS where it had rested, to the Department of Justice, In The Homeland Security Act of 2002 transferred some of the duties of this bureau to Homeland Security (6 U.S.C. 531).

BOARDS

EXECUTIVE OFFICE FOR IMMIGRATION REVIEW

Through three administrative tribunals, The Board of Immigration Appeals, The office of the Chief Immigration Judge, and The Office of the Chief Administrative

Hearing Officer, the Department of Justice manages the processes of appeals for immigration cases.

UNITED STATES PAROLE COMMISSION

This Board makes recommendations and decisions for Federal Parole Hearings. The Board also monitors and creates policies for release and standards for releases to be considered.

OFFICE OF THE COMMUNITY ORIENTED POLICING SERVICES

This Office actively is involved in research, development and advising of the nations police forces to increase the use of community oriented policing.

FOREIGN CLAIMS SETTLEMENT COMMISSION OF THE UNITED STATES

This is a quasi independent judicial agency within the Department of Justice which handles cases involving immigrants and foreign governments.

LABOR

The Department of Labor was established by Act in 1913.(29 U.S.C. 551) to foster, promote and develop the welfare of the wage earners of the United States. To improve working conditions and to advance opportunities for profitable employment is the goal. First established as part of the Department of the Interior in 1884 by Act, the department became a bureau for Department of Commerce and Labor created by Act in 1903 (15 U.S. C. 1501, : 20 U.S. C. note).

The Department is under charge of the Secretary of Labor who is the chief advisor to the President about labor matters.

SECRETARY

The Secretary of Labor is the advisor to the President. The Secretary develops, implements and enforces the nations labor policies to "advance the profitable employment" of the people on the soils of the United States of America.

EMPLOYEES COMPENSATION APPEALS BOARD

This is a quasi judicial, three person Board that makes the final decisions for the Federal Workers Compensation appeals. Created as part of 1946 Reorganization Plan No. 2 (60 Stat.1095) This Board has final say on the matters of fact and law in review on appeal for the limited cases they are responsible to decide.

ADMINISTRATIVE REVIEW BOARD

This Board consists of up to five Board members, who are appointed by the Secretary to adjudicate appeals cases arising out of the McNamara O'Hara Service Contract Act and the Davis Bacon Act. Board decisions may be appealed in Federal District or Appellate Courts.

BENEFITS REVIEW BOARD

A five member Board, appointed by the Secretary adjudicates appeals under the Longshore and Harbor Worker's Compensation Act and Black Lung Benefits Act, the decisions may be appealed to Federal District or Appellate Courts.

OFFICE OF SMALL BUSINESS PROGRAMS

This Office ensures procurement opportunities for small business, and has special procurement opportunities for disabled, minority, women owned businesses, HUBZone businesses, and businesses owned by service disabled veterans. This office handles issues under the Small Business Regulatory Enforcement Act and the central referral point for inquiries and complaints under this Act. This office also oversees Island colleges and small business issues, and colleges and university programs and facility awareness to the targeted small business owners.

OFFICE OF JOB CORPS

This office involves their mission to attract young adults teach them relevant skills to help them become employable and independent. There are six regional offices included in this office.

THE SOLICITOR OF LABOR

Provides legal advice and research to the Department of Labor as requested.

WOMEN'S BUREAU

This Bureau is responsible for promoting the status of wage earning women, improving working conditions for women, and increasing the efficiency and advancement of opportunities in the workplace.

INTERNATIONAL AFFAIRS

This Bureau is mandated to carry out the international duties of the Secretary of Labor. To develop policies, activities and coordinate international activities involving the United States and foreign governments in labor issues, governmental and non-governmental.

OFFICE OF THE INSPECTOR GENERAL

The Office of the Inspector General conducts audits and evaluations to review the DOL programs and operations for efficiency, economics, and integrity as they are involved within the DOL and with other agencies and non-governmental contracts.

EMPLOYMENT AND TRAINING ADMINISTRATION

Provides quality job training, employment and labor markets related to the Federal, State and workforce labor programs.

OFFICE OF WORKFORCE INVESTMENT

Provides leadership, oversight, and policy review and advice to the Nation's workforce employers and governmental offices and agencies. Provides information, and details how to keep up with technology, tools, career guidance skills, and competencies in a variety of workplaces.

BUSINESS RELATIONS GROUP

Provides training and advice to implement the President;s High Growth Training initiative which prepares workers to take advantage of new and increasing job opportunities in high growth workforce areas.

OFFICE OF WORKFORCE SECURITY

Is responsible for leadership, advice, oversight, policy guidance, funding applications, and technical assistance for the Federal – State unemployment compensation program. Federal workforce legislative requirements are upheld through directives from this office.

OFFICE OF NATIONAL RESPONSE

This office is responsible for administrating the National Trade Adjustment Assistance and the National Emergency Grant programs for displaced workers.

OFFICE OF APPRENTICESHIP

Operates the National Registered Apprenticeship System to promote the adoption by employers, labor and other organizations for formalized apprentice and training programs in high growth workforce areas. This office also administrates the same programs for minorities and women apprenticeship programs.

OFFICE OF FOREIGN LABOR CERTIFICATION

Performs the regulations, and certifications required for foreign immigrants seeking admission to the United States.

OFFICE OF PERFORMANCE AND TECHNOLOGY

Responsible for the construction, maintenance and improvement of the ETA's technology infrastructure for the national and regional offices, this office provides the executive leadership with to provide 21st century information technology to support the Agency's mission and all their business lines and sites.

OFFICE OF POLICY DEVELOPMENT AND RESEARCH

Provides advice, policy and research to improve the ETA's ability to improve the public workforce.

Supports the OPDR with advisories and policies to increase the service and suggested improvements to the public workforce. This office analyzes, formulates, and recommends legislative changes and options for change to improve the public workforce.

OFFICE OF FINANCIAL AND ADMINISTRATIVE MANAGEMENT

This office serves the ETA with leadership, guidance, policy advice for internal and external financial management.

OFFICE OF REGIONAL INNOVATION AND TRANSORMATION

Provides through six regional offices, the supportive development and innovation in the workforce investment system through oversight, and administration improvement, and to detail the outcomes of taxpayer funded studies and programs funded to keep the DOL and the ETA and the workers in the 21st Century of work technology and training.

EMPLOYEE BENEFITS SECURITY ADMINISTRATION

This Administration promotes the pension, health and other benefits of over 150 million participants in over 6 million private sector employee benefit plans. This administration was established through The Employee Retirement Income Security Act enforced through 15 EBSA offices.

EMPLOYMENT STANDARDS ADMINISTRATION

Handles such Congress Act benefits and standards as passed. Includes benefits, and minimum wage oversight and implementation policy and advice. The Contracts office of the Contract Compliance Programs administers and enforced three equal opportunity mandates established by Executive Order 11246, as amended section 503 of the Rehabilitation Act of the 1973. This office also enforces the US. Vietnam War Veterans Readjustment Assistance Act of 1974 as amended (38 U.S.C. 4212) to ensure war veterans are given priority for Federal contracts.

WAGES

This office controls the implementation and oversight of wages and hours that are involved in Federal Labor Legislative Mandates. A large variety of types of issues have been mandated by legislation. This office develops training and advisories to facilitate businesses in compliance.

LABOR MANAGEMENT STANDARDS

This office conducts criminal and civil investigations to safeguard the integrity of union and to ensure union democracy and conducts its own investigations covered under the Labaor Management Reporting and Disclosure Act.

WORKERS COMPENSATION

This office is responsible for Federal worker's compensation programs for Federal employees, maritime employees, and employment on all navigated waters in the United States, as well as coal miners disabled by coal dust, to survivors of those killed in mine disasters.

OCCUPATIONAL SAFETY AND HEALTH ADMINISTRATION

OSHA sets and enforces workplace health and safety standards. OSHA also assists employers in meeting and maintaining those standards.

Established by Act in 1970 (29 U.S.C. 651 et seq) to have a four fold regulation over employee workplace safety and healthful environments in the workplace, as well as to provide the consumers with safe and healthfully prepared or produced products (this is NOT food safety or health inspectors, that is a separate division in the Department of Agriculture) To provide programs for employees to reach out for assistance when necessary.

MINE SAFETY AND HEALTH ADMINISTRATION

This office was established to address the same issues as OSHA in all mines in the United States of America. This office implements all legislative mandates, conducts its own investigations and can recommend criminal or civil proceedings against the mine operators and owners.

OFFICE OF DISABILITY EMPLOYMENT POLICY

This office oversees implementation and advises on mandatory legislation to all employers, public or private that hire the disabled, including the legal mandates on hiring disabled persons to meet the mandates of equal opportunity employment , the Department of Health and Human Services oversees the Division of Americans with Disabilities Act for other areas of labor oversight for Disabled workers.

BUREAU OF LABOR STATISTICS

This Bureau is charged with keeping records, statistics, doing research and reports as requested, and providing advisories as requested by the Department of Labor bureaus, offices, Secretary or other government agencies, and private businesses.

VETERANS EMPLOYMENT AND TRAINING SERVICE

This office is charged with all aspects of training and employment as mandated in legislation to be the responsibility of the Department of Labor. These services cross over for Active duty, and Guard workers as well. The Department of Defense and the VA also have divisions for veteran's employment and training. This office makes sure all mandated legislation for those offices is appropriately trained to the divisions required to meet those new mandates, or changes in mandated legislations in existence.

STATE

Established by Act of 1789, the Department of Foreign Affairs was renamed the Department of State by Act of 11789 (22 U.S.C. 2651). The Department of State is the chief advisor in policy and execution of foreign affairs policy to the President. The goal is to promote the long range security and well being of The United States of America.

REGIONAL BUREAUS

Foreign affairs worldwide are handled by many regional bureaus, which are divided into specific areas of expertise in each area.

ADMINISTRATION

The bureau of Administration for Department of State is similar to the Office of Administration for the Department of Defense. This office does the paperwork, procurement, contracts and other office work necessary to the regional offices and oversees the regional office Administration duties done at their own geographic locations.

CONSULAR AFFAIRS

This office is responsible for the interests of citizens abroad, Their safety and the ensuring of citizens immigrating or other issues as far as they concern the Department of State. Approximately 18 million passports a year are issues to facilitate border crossing and citizen identification and whereabouts.

DEMOCRACY, HUMAN RIGHTS AND LABOR

This office is responsible for developing and implementing US policies on human rights and labor in foreign countries, both for American citizens and those who work for American owned or import receiving companies of products and services sold in the United States of America. A LOT more is said about this office in later chapters.

DIPLOMATIC SECURITY

This office coordinates security for American diplomats, whether working or visiting foreign countries. (This office has come under increasing fire for their handling of Benghazi Embassy).

ECONCONOMICS, ENERGY AND BUSINESS AFFAIRS

This office is charged with developing and implementing as well as researching, documenting and advising other Executive and Federal agencies and offices regarding trade, agreements, problems, and policy to uphold the US Labor and Trade Standards, among other issues involved in international trade.

EDUCATIONAL AND CULTURAL AFFAIRS

Established under the Mutual Cultural and Educational Exchange Act, The Fullbright-Hays Act, this office promotes, develops and implements programs under each of these acts to further cultural and educational sharing and tolerance.

FOREIGN MISSIONS

This office operates all the vehicles, taxes, and support for travel programs for the officials and staff of the Department of State.

FOREIGN SERVICE INSTITUTE

This Institute is the primary training division of the Department of State to train and inform all branches and divisions of current legislation, goals, programs, implementation guidelines and advisories for those in a particular foreign office or service workplace.

INFORMATION RESOURCE MANAGEMENT

The division provides the necessary technical equipment, services, support, interactions and needs of the Department of State as requested by the Secretary or the Administration Office of the Department of State.

INSPECTOR GENERAL

This office conducts independent audits, inspections and investigations to provide the oversight the Department of State as well as to respond to complaints or allegations brought to the Inspector General for investigation by the President, The Secretary, or through them from Congress or other Federal branches of government and their bureaus and agencies as applicable.

INTELLIGENCE AND RESEARCH

This bureau coordinates all activities with the other intelligence branches of several areas of government as applied to foreign policy, foreign relations and providing for the safety and security of State Department activities

.

INTERNATIONAL INFORMATION PROGRAMS

This office inter-relates with several Federal Departments, as well as foreign government agencies that are in the similar description of mandatory duties to ensure safety and good communications at all time between governments and the daily critical status of foreign land areas. This office provides advice and research as requested by the Secretary of State, and through the Secretary, the President and Congress at all times.

INTERNATIONAL NARCOTICS AND LAW ENFORCEMENT

This agency is charged with the communications and partnering between the United States and INTERPOL, as well as foreign governments to reduce illegal drug trafficking and establish and implement programs to meet narcotics and law enforcement policies of the Department of State, as mandated by Congress.

INTERNATIONAL ORGANIZATIONS

This office is charged with knowing, researching, and keeping the Department of State Secretary, and offices as required to create conferences, implement United States participation and safety for conferences requested, and all aspects of keeping the Secretary and Department of State aware of the policies and keeps constant research on changes that will change interactions between the United States and foreign governments.

INTERNATIONAL SECURITY AND NONPROLIFERATION

This office does much of the actual planning and implementing of relations as defined by other divisions and agreed to by the Secretary. This office is responsible for the research, oversight, and constant data and information to ensure the nonproliferation agreements are being adhered to by all countries to monitor the build up or reduction of weapons as mandated in treaties.

LEGAL ADVISOR

The office of the Legal Advisor is the branch of the Department of State that has a staff of lawyers who keep the other offices and bureaus constantly updated and informed, and as requested provide legal advisories on situations involving the Department of State.

MEDICAL SERVICES

This office is charged with the duty to provide medical support, and healthcare for foreign State Department employees and administrators as requested. This office also is responsible to ensure all traveling dignitaries have adequate medical emergency staff for any situation that may arise while in route, or in foreign countries.

OCEANS AND INTERNATIONAL ENVIRONMENTAL AND SCIENTIFIC AFFAIRS

This office keeps the State Department in all foreign countries, waters and international oceans waters up to date and current on all situations that arise concerning the Department of State. This office works to increase Environmental and Scientific policy agreements to enhance the stated policies of the United States of America in dealing with foreign business or government interactions.

OVERSEAS BUILDING OPERATIONS

This office oversees, researches, implements and request what manpower, materials, and security are needed to maintain safe buildings for Department of State around the globe.

POLITICAL-MILITARY AFFAIRS

This office is the liaison between the military and the political branches of the United States foreign service and citizens who are under the auspices of the office of Consular affairs. This office will be discussed in later chapters in relation to Behnghazi.

POPULATION, REFUGEES AND MIGRATION

This office maintains records, oversight, and help for Americans in relation to any of these areas in foreign countries, as well as being responsible to report to the government their constantly updated data on the populations of those countries, the stability of the government at all times, and the status of refugees and those who want to migrate with the assistance of the United States Department of State, or to America.

PROTOCOL

This office has the duty to ensure that when any State Department Secretary or employee is in any foreign country they are well aware of not just the protocol expected in relation to the other country's citizens and government, but also of the protocols for all aspects of their own job. This office keeps a constant update, and advisory ability on issues such as what is diplomatic immunity and how much it will cover, and then ensures all persons needing this knowledge are well trained to be safe, keep the State Department facilities safe, and to keep America out of critical issues from created by not knowing, or not following protocol.

RESOURCES MANAGEMENT

This office manages all the resources belonging to the American taxpayers purchased for and used by the Department of State. Procurements, and maintaining the facilities are included in the vast resources management of global relations facilities of the Department of State. This office also manages all facilities resources of Department of State facilities and programs on American soil.

VERIFICATION, COMPLIANCE AND IMPLEMENTATION

This office is in charge of verifying that protocol, procedures, and management are in compliance and to oversee implementation of projects and programs as required.

FOREIGN SERVICE

The Foreign Service office is charged with the actual staffing and personnel needs of the Department of State workers, administrators and contracted workers while on State Department assignments.

TRANSPORTATION

Under the umbrella of 11 administrations the Department of Transportation sets, administrates, implements and oversees the nations transportation systems. The Federal Department of Transportation is responsible to interact and advice, and support State transportation systems as well. Established by Act of October 1966 ((49 U.S.C. 102 and 102 note) to assure the coordinated effect on administration of the transportation in the United States of America and to develop international transportation programs and policies.

SECRETARY OF TRANSPORTATION

The Secretary of Transportation is appointed to be the Principal advisor to the President on Federal Transportation programs

AVIATION AND INTERNATIONAL AFFAIRS

This office with the Undersecretary of Aviation at its head, develops, reviews, and coordinates policy for relating to the economic regulation of the airline industry and international affair related to aviation travel between the United States and foreign airlines, and foreign airports.

DRUG, ALCOHOL POLICY AND COMPLIANCE

This office develops and implements policy for airline carriers, pilots, and passengers in relation to drug, alcohol and ensures compliance through continuance of drug testing, in department education programs and policies.

INTELLIGENCE, SECURITY AND EMERGENCY RESPONSE

This office sets, implements and ensures compliance in the airline industry in intelligence, the use of intelligence for the safety of the airline industry, and sets, trains and ensures emergency response programs are in place, prepared and at readiness for any occurrence in the airline industry.

TRANSPORTATION POLICY

The office of Assistant Secretary for Transportation for Policy sets, and advises on policy. Develops, trains, and oversees policy is being in compliance for the safety of all in the airline industry.

FEDERAL AVIATION ADMINISTRATION

This office is the office that implements the policies for the airline industry. Established by Federal Act of 1958 *72 Stat.731) the FAA was added to the Department of Transportation to regulate civil aviation and US commercial air space, to maintain and operate air traffic control and navigation systems for both civil and military aircrafts and to develop and administrate the Federal Airspace programs and air travel.

FEDERAL HIGHWAY ADMINISTRATION

This office was established by the Department of Transportation Act (49 U.S.C. 104) to be responsible for the nations Federal highways and to work with State highway administrations to ensure highway travel in the United States. This office also partners with other nations to develop and implement highway systems that interface with United States systems and interests.

FEDERAL RAILROAD ADMINISTRATION

Established in 1966 pursuant to Section 3 (e)(1) of the Department of Transportation Act (49 U.S.C. 103) to create and enforce regulations of all rail activity on the Federal Railroad transit authority.

NATIONAL HIGHWAY TRAFFIC SAFETY ADMINISTRATION

Established in 1970 by Act (23 U.S.C. 401 note) to help increase highway safty across the nations roadways. Research, development, and enforcement policies, protocols, implementation and compliance oversight are included in the NHTSA.

FEDERAL TRANSIT ADMINISTRATION

Established by Section 1 of the Reorganization Plan 2 of 1968 (5 U.S.C. app 1) the Federal Transit Administration is charged with assisting in development of improved mass transit systems. To advise and encourage the financing of approved plans for better national transit.

MARITIME ADMINITRATION

Established by the Reorganization Plan No 21 of 1950 (5 U.S.C. app) the Maritime Administration was Act of 1981 (46 U.S.C. 1601) transferred the Maritime Administration to the Department of Transportation. This office develops policy, rules, regulations, international policy and protocols for vessels in American waters, and American vessels in open water, and on American waters. This Administration monitors and approves ship yard and shipping construction and repair costs to maintain the nations maritime capabilities.

SAINT LAWRENCE SEAWAY DEVELOPMENT CORPORATIONS

This office was initiated by the Saint Lawrence Seaway Development Corporation seaway Act of 1954 (33 U.S.C. 981-990) and was changed to a part of the Department of Transportation by Act in 1966. This office is charged with the safety and open operating of the Saint Lawrence channel between the United States and Canada.

PIPELINE AND HAZARDOUS MATERIALS SAFETY ADMINISTRATION

Established February 20, 2005, this office does not list an Act or a defined reason for its existence. This office is charged with the guarantee of safety of hazardous materials and pipeline safety across this nation. Much more about this in a later chapter.

RESEARCH AND INNOVATIVE TECHNOLOGY ADMINISTRATION

This office is charged with research and creating new and innovative technological systems for all departments of the Department of Transportation for improving safety in all areas of transportation. Established by Act under the Norman Y Mineta Research and Special Programs Improvement act (49 U.S.C.101 note).This office provides strategic directives and oversight of DOT's Intelligent Transportation Systems.

FEDERAL MOTOR CARRIER SAFETY ADMINISTRATION

Established in 2000 by Act this office pursuant to the 1999 Motor Carrier Act (49 U.S.C. 113) to prevent motor vehicle related fatalities and injuries involving commercial carriers. This office investigates, creates standards, researches and implements programs designed to increase Motor Carrier Safety.

SURFACE TRANSPORTATION BOARD

Established by the Interstate Commerce Commission in 1996, pursuant to the 1995 Termination Act (40 U.S.C. 10101 et seq) as an independent adjudicatory body within the department of Transportation. This office is charged with matters formerly under the jurisdiction of the Interstate Commerce Commission to investigate, and resolve disputes among the states, carriers, and ensure oversight on all surface transportation safety regulation.

DEPARTMENT OF THE TREASURY

A very troubling statement is at the beginning of this Department. It is the statement that in year 2004, the year of The Manual of the United States Government that was used for this synopsis, the Department did not meet its deadline in submitting its paperwork for the manual publication for the year. There was at least one other agency that failed to submit mandatory submission. (There will be greater discussion of this subject in another chapter in this book, however, the word MANDATORY is easily defined by looking at any dictionary. It is not discretionary, or maybe, might, or possibly, the failure of people paid by the taxpayers to do a job that is mandated by law is disturbing).

The Department of the Treasury performs four basic functions:
formulating and recommending economic, financial, tax and fiscal policies
and serving as the financial agent for the United States,
enforcing the laws,
and minting of coins, and currency.

SECRETARY

The Treasury Department was established by Act of September 1789 (31 U.S.C. 301 and 301 note). Many Acts over the centuries have formed and shaped the Department as it is today.

The Secretary is the major policy advisor to the President on finance, with responsibility for formulating and recommending domestic and international financial, economic and tax policies among many other duties listed below. The Department of

Treasury is the United States major law enforcement agent for financial laws, and policies.

ALCOHOL AND TOBACCO TAX AND TRADE BUREAU

This office is responsible for the economic and tax policies for the United States of America.

BUREAU OF THE COMPTROLLER OF THE CURRENCY

This office was established in February 1863 (12 Stat. 665) . The stated mission is to regulate national banks. The Comptroller is appointed for a 5 year term by the President with the advice and consent of the Senate. This office takes applications and investigates to approve or disapprove of new banks, and oversees all banks for compliance to the Federal banking mandates.

BUREAU OF ENGRAVING AND PRINTING

This office was established by Act in July 1862 (31 U.S. C. 103) and has the same duties, that since 1950 have been financed by Public Law 81-656 which established a revolving fund. The office is run by a Director appointed by the Secretary of the Treasury. This office designs, prints and finishes all the of the paper currency and many other security documents, including White House invitations and military identification cards. This office advises and assists other government offices and agencies with document design and printing as requested.

FINANCIAL MANAGEMENT SERVICE

This office provides a central accounting authority for Federal programs, agencies, as well as operates the Federal collections programs.

INTERNAL REVENUE SERVICE

The IRS was established by act of July 1862 (26U.S.C.7802. This agency is responsible for administering and enforcing the internal revenue laws and provisions. The mission is to collect the appropriate taxes from all mandated sources at the least cost to the taxpayers.

UNITED STATES MINT

The United States Mint utilizes the designs and works with the Bureau of Engraving and Printing to produce an adequate volume of circulating coinage to the United States to conduct its trade and commerce. Established by Act in April 17792 (1 Stat 246) it was re-codified on September 13 1980 (31 U.S.C. 304, 5131) and additionally changed from Bureau of Mint by Secretarial order of January 9, 1984.

BUREAU OF PUBLIC DEBT

This office was established on June 30, 940 pursuant to the Reorganization act of 1939 (31 U.S.C. 306). This office is charged with borrow money needed to operate the federal government .and provide reimbursable support to Federal agencies. Through Treasury Bills, bonds, notes, and the U.S. Savings Bond Programs the Bureau of Public Debt seeks to raise funds for needed programs as requested by the President and Congress.

OFFICE OF THRIFT SUPERVISION

Created by the Financial Institutions Act of 1989 the office of Thrift Supervision was established ot effectively and efficiently supervise thrift institutions in the United states. Headed by a Director appointed by the President with the advice and consent of the Senate, the office is the primary advisory office to the President, and the Secretary of the Treasury on thrift institutions.

DEPARTMENT OF VETERANS AFFAIRS

The Department of Veterans Affairs was established as an executive administration by the Veterans Affairs Act (38 U.S.C. 201, note) The mission, as stated is: operates programs to benefit veterans and members of their families. The VA did not meet the deadline for submission to the 2004 Manual of the United States Government. There will an extended discussion of the VA in other chapters in this book.

ACTIVITIES

The Veterans Administration has a large number of mandated services for veterans.

CEMETARIES

The VA operates free burial cemeteries and maintains them across the nation.

CENTER FOR MINORITY VETERANS

The Center was established by Public Law 103-446 (108 Stat 4645) and is responsible for promoting services to minority veterans.

CENTER FOR WOMEN VETERANS

This Center was established by Public Law 103-446 (108 Stat 4645) and is responsible for promoting services to women veterans.

HEALTH SERVICES

Health services is called the Veterans Health Administration to provide hospital, clinical, home and domiciliary care and outpatient medical and dental care to veterans.

VETERANS BENEFITS

The Veterans Benefits office provides information, advice and assistance to veterans, their dependents, beneficiaries, representatives and other as mandated by law.

VETERANS APPEALS

The Veterans Appeals Board is responsible for entering the final appellate decisions of entitlement and for deciding attorney fees that can be charged for cases.

FIELD FACILITIES

The Department has several field facilities to handle the veteran matters across the nation. Hospitals, clinics, cemeteries and all other VA buildings are overseen by this office.

INDEPENDENT ESTABLISHMENTS AND GOVERNMENT CORPORATIONS:

These are offices and independent facilities that are included in the auspices of the United States Government, but are not Departments of the Executive office.

AFRICAN DEVELOPMENT FOUNDATION

To alleviate poverty and establish sustainable development and empowerment in Africa, to expand local capacity to promote and support grassroots economic endeavors. in Africa is the mission of this Foundation . . Established by Act 22 *22 U.S.C. 290h) this office works to support self help efforts in Africa.

BROADCASTING BOARD OF GOVERNORS

The sole mission of this Board is: to promote freedom and democracy and to enhance understanding by media to accurate, objective and balanced news and information about the US, and the world to audiences abroad. Established in 1999 by Act these activities are directed by an eight member board appointed by the President.

CIA

The CIA was established in the NSA Security Act of 1947 (50 U.S. C. 40 et seq) and was changed to function under the Executive Order (December 4, 1981) 12333 (There is considerable debate as to the legality of this change without full Congress knowledge and public approval by the citizens of the United States of America) and changed again in the Intelligence Reform and Terrorism Prevention Act of 2004 (50 U.S. C. 401 note) along with Executive Orders, regulations and directives. These are all being reviewed in 2013 and 2014 as citizens have expressed severe disapproval of what has been done under these changes. The CIA is supposed to collect, evaluate, and disseminate vital information on political, military, economic, scientific and other developments to protect national security. There are now other agencies involved in these investigations, which have many citizens, as well as some Congresspersons questioning the Constitutionality of some of the invasions of persons private lives without warrant, or public hearing.

COMMODITY FUTURES TRADING COMMISSION

The purpose of this agency is to protect market users and the general public from fraud, manipulation and abusive practices related to the sale of commodity futures and options and to foster open, competitive and financially sound commodity futures and option markets. Established by Act The commodity Futures Trading Commission Act of 1974 (7 U.S.C. 4a) and renewed by Congress in 1978, 1982, 1986, 1992, 1995 and 2000). A quick check of their website ensures the Commission is still in existence, I called and left a message to find out why there is no Regional Office beyond Kansas City to the west. (There will be further discussion of this office in later chapters).

CONSUMER PRODUCT SAFETY COMMISSION

This Commission was established as an independent regulatory agency by the Consumer Public Safety Act (15 U.S.C. 2014 et seq) to as stated in their mission: protect the public against unreasonable risks of injury from consumer products. This commission promotes research and investigation into the safety of products, works with the states to minimize conflicting regulations regarding products, and to ensure that there is oversight into the causes and create prevention programs for product related deaths, illnesses and injuries. The Commission consists of three members appointed by the President for terms of seven years. Questions and concerns may be researched or addressed on their website. A LOT more will be said about this agency in other chapters. THIS is one of the most important commissions and needs to have strict oversight to make sure corruption is not any part of the findings of the commission as their findings are utilized for safety standards, and to advise the President and Congress on critical consumer dangers.

NOTE: July 26, 2017, this Commission needs to be well known to citizens and the voters need to be watchful of what this Commission is doing in response to real life and death complaints of consumers, and active cases by States, and Federal prosecutors on behalf of the consumers. The recent cases involving motor vehicles that were KNOWN to have been defective, but the recalls either not sent, or were delayed, or were hidden from the public and the government have given important impetus to the need for this commission to be active and up to date.

Medications that have now been found to be the major source of drug addiction as they are either opiates or synthetic opiates and prescribed without concern for the subsequent addiction of the consumes have also pointed to the need for this commission as a fast and efficient over sight to the FDA and CDC agencies in watch dogging foods, drugs, and any item that can harm consumers. The incident of pet foods some years ago being filled with plastic shavings from another country where well known pet and stock food sellers in the United States was not found until the bags of pellets had been sold and fed to stock animals that were already slaughtered and sold to consumers also indicates the importance of this Commission to be cutting edge in keeping our consumers safe.

CORPORATION FOR NATIONAL AND COMMUNITY SERVICE

Established in 1993, this is one of the nicest and most American heritage of all the agencies. Volunteering is an American concept that has spread throughout the world. Many other countries had wonderful people who volunteer, care about others, and have public secular and religious groups that help others, but the concept of Americans helping each other has been long and growing since the old barn raising day and the well established concepts of Native American culture to help others. Thanksgiving is a celebration of those two cultures coming together and each year reminds of that we can accomplish amazing goals together and helping each other.

Established by Act in 1993 The National and Community Service Trust Act of 1993 (42 U.S.C. 1265) created this agency to create new community programs and encourage involvement in national and community service. The website is extensive and there is contact information that helps anyone join, or advance national and community service.

DEFENSE NUCLEAR FACILITIES SAFETY BOARD

Established by Act as an Independent agency on September 29,1988 by the Atomic Energy Act of 1954 as amended (42 U.S.C. 2286-2286i). This Board reviews and evaluates the content and implementation of standards in the design, construction, operation and decommissioning of nuclear facilities for the Department of Energy.

ENVIRONMENTAL PROTCTION AGENCY

Established by Reorganization Plan 3 of 1970 as an independent agency, the EPA is charged with promoting human health and to safeguard the natural environment, air, water, and land upon which life depends.

The EPA covers air, water, radiation issues, solid waste and emergency response as it applies to waste and environmental safety, This agency provides advise, and support for public and private programs to know the law and to adhere to the law, and well as enforcing the compliance with EPA standards.

There are two major areas that citizens need to read and learn about the EPA. First of all, as it is listed in the Manual of The United States Government as an independent agency, the EPA can not whimsically be removed or dictated to by any of the three branches of government. The enabling legislation that brought any agency into being MUST be PUBLICLY announced BEFORE Congress can begin to investigate or evaluate changes. IF the citizens do NOT want the changes, it is their DUTY to make sure their CONGRESSPERSONS know that they will be recalled, or not re-elected if they do not follow the demands of the PEOPLE who they serve.

Second: the citizens have a duty to DEMAND that the EPA keep them healthy and safe. July 26, 2017, it was announced in California that NEW EPA standards will be enforced in behalf of neighboring communities. While EPA is Federal, that is a good model. The EPA needs to establish danger and demand that companies, or municipal energy entities clean up or close. There have been several severe leaks in at least one major energy facility forcing hundreds of citizens to evacuate and stay out of their homes for months.

EQUAL EMPOLOYMENT OPPORTUNITIES COMMISSION

This agency was established by the Civil Rights (Title VII) Act of 1964 (42 U.S.C. 2000e-4) and became operational in July 1965. The duty of this Commission is to research, advise, implement and enforce the laws of the United States of America in regards to no discrimination based on race, color, religion, sex, national origin, disability or age. There will be a longer discussion on this agency in later chapters).

EXPORT-IMPORT BANK OF THE UNITED STATES

Established by the Export-Import Bank Act of 1934 and now operating under authority of the Export-Import Bank Act of 1945 as amended (12 U.S.C. 635 et seq) this office is charged with to create and maintain U.S. private sector jobs by financing exports of the nation's goods and services. The service is expected to secure a reasonable expectation of repayment before financing any aspect requested for exporting or importing from private companies.

FARM CREDIT ADMINISTRATION

Established in 1933 by Executive Order 6084 . The office conducts examinations of the various Farm Credit institutions, and examines the organizations owned by the Farm Credit lending institutions, as well as the National Cooperative Bank.

FEDERAL COMMUNICATIONS COMMISSION

Established by the Federal Communications Act of 1934 (47 U.S.C. 31 et seq) to regulate interstate and foreign communications by television, radio, wire, satellite, and cable, as well as rapid, and efficient nationwide, worldwide telephone and telegraph services.

FEDERAL DEPOSIT INSURANCE CORPORATION

Established by the Banking Act of 1933, this agency promotes the safety of private investment in banks by insuring accounts up to $100,000 as well as examining the banks and savings institutions regularly.

FEDERAL ELECTION COMMISSION

Established by the Federal Election Campaign Act of 1971 (2 U.S.C. 437c) the
Commission has exclusive jurisdiction in the administration and civil enforcement of
laws regulating the acquisition and expenditure of campaign funds to ensure compliance
by participants with Federal campaign law.

This is an interesting agency, that again, established by an ACT of Congress, has
the power to do its job. Researching and learning the supportive material is the right and
DUTY of all citizens to make sure this Commission is NOT detoured from its duty by
any source.

In the most recent election it was well established that the VOTERS are angry and
upset over campaign antics of both parties, and want them stopped. The VOTERS need
to petition and DEMAND that the FEC investigate and create suggested legislation to
support better enforcement and over sight of campaign funding and where those funds
come from.

The FEC, like any agency in the Manual of The United States Government was
legislated at the demand of the PEOPLE, and its enabling legislation by the Congress that
put it in place can NOT be whimsically changed. PUBLIC hearings must be heard, and
as noted many times in this book, VOTERS have the RIGHT and DUTY to let their
Congressperson know that if they do NOT support the rights and demands of the
PEOPLE, they will be recalled, or not re-elected.

FEDERAL HOUSING FINANCE BOARD

Established by the Federal Home Loan Bank Act as amended (12 U.S.C. 1421 et
seq) as an independent agency to ensure the safety and soundness of the Federal Home
Loan Banks, their access to the capital market and the fulfillment of the housing finance
missions. Federal Home Loan Banks are privately capitalized, government sponsored

enterprises, created to stimulate the mortgage financing and provide liquidity to the credit market of the United States.

FEDERAL LABOR RELATIONS BOARD

Established by the Reorganization Plan 2 of 1978 (5 U.S.C. app) consolidates the central policymaking functions in the Federal Labor Management relations The duties are mandated in Title VII (Federal Service Labor-Management Relations) to administer the law that protects the right of employees of the Federal Government to organize, bargain collectively, and participate in labor organizations of their own choosing.

FEDERAL MARITIME COMMISSION

Established in 1963 by the Reorganization Plan No. 2 (46 U.S.C. 301-307) the Maritime Commission regulates shipping under specific statutes. There are a number of areas that are overseen, policies set, and implemented and overseen for compliance by the maritime companies as covered in those specific statutes.

FEDERAL MEDIATION AND CONCILIATION SERVICE

Established by the Labor Relations-Management Act of 1947 (29 U.S.C. 172 this agency is charged with assisting labor and management to come to agreements without strikes or law suits that disrupt service to the public or any Federal agency.

FEDERAL MINE SAFETY AND HEALTH REVIEW COMMISSION

Established by the Federal Mine Safety and Health Act of 1977 (30 U.S.C. 801) this agency is an independent adjudicative agency to enforce Mine Safety and Health Review Commission mandates for the nation's metal, coal, and non-metal mines.

FEDERAL RESERVE SYSTEMS

Established by the Federal Reserve Act of 1913 (12 U.S.C. 221) the Federal Reserve Bank is charged to set policy and to ensure compliance with the nation's banking regulations. The Board of Governors who oversee the FRS are a seven member Board appointed by the President with the advice and consent of the Senate. The Chairman of the Board of Reserves is a member of the National Advisory Council on International Monetary and Financial Policies.

FEDERAL RETIREMENT THRIFT INVESTMENT BOARD

Established as an independent agency by the Federal Employees Retirement System Act of 1986 (5 U.S.C. 8351-8379) the five board members, one of whom is designated chairman, are appointed by the President with the advice and consent of the Senate. This is part time position. This Board oversees and protects the Federal Employees retirement investment accounts.

FEDERAL TRADE COMMISSION

Established in 1914 by the Federal Trade Commission Act (15 U.S.C. 41-58 this Commission is charged wit the jurisdiction to enhance consumer welfare and protect competition in broad sectors of the economy. The five member board is appointed by the President with consent and advice from the Senate for a term of 7 years.

GENERAL SERVICES COMMISSION

Established by the Federal Property and Administrative Services Act of 1949 (40 U.S.C. 751) this office charged with the establishing of policy and administration of the government's property and assets. Procurement, oversight of property, and dealing with contract disputes over materials and services sold to the Federal Government or received from the Federal Government. Some government agencies have their own materials, services and procurement offices.

INTER-AMERICAN FOUNDATION

Established in 1969 by Act (22 U.S.C. 2900) as an experimental U. S. Foreign assistance program this Foundation is a nine member Board, appointed by the President with consent and approval of the Senate, this agency supports social and economic development in Latin America and The Caribbean by use of grants to local self help programs.

MERIT SYSTEMS PROTECTION BOARD

Established by Act of 1883 (22 Stat. 403) Reorganization Plan No. 2 of 1978 (15 U.S.C. app) redesignated part of the commission as the Merit Systems Protection Board to protect the integrity of the Federal Personnel merit systems and the rights of Federal Employees.

NASA

Established by the National Aeronautics and Space Act of 1958 as amended (42 U.S.C. 2451 et seq) the mission of NASA is to pioneer the future in space exploration, discovery and research in aeronautics.

NATIONAL ARCHIVES AND RECORDS ADMINISTRATION

Charged with the safeguarding and preservation of the records of the United States of America the NARA is the successor to the National Archives Establishment which was established in 1984 by Act (44 U.S.C. 2101 et seq).

NATIONAL CAPITAL PLANNING COMMISSION

Established by Act of 1984 as amended (40 U.S.C. 71 et seq) NCPC is charged as the central agency for planning and development activities for Federal lands in the National Capital Regions.

NATIONAL CREDIT UNION ADMINISTRATION

Established by Act of 1970 (12 U.S.C. 1752) and reorganized by Act of 1978 (12 U.S.C. 226) as an independent agency. The mission of the NCUA is to charter, insure , supervise, and examine Federal Credit Unions and Administrate the National Credit Union Share Insurance Fund.

NATIONAL FOUNDATION ON THE ARTS AND THE HUMANITIES

Established by the Arts and Humanities Act of 1965 (20 U.S.C. 951) the NFAH is charged with the development and promotion of a broadly conceived policy of support for the arts and humanities in the United States of America and for institutions that preserve cultural heritage in the United States of America.

NATIONAL ENDOWMENT FOR THE ARTS

Established in 1965 by Congress, the National Endowment for the Arts is charged with the advancement of the arts in education and dedicated to excellence in the Arts and preservation of arts in the United States.

NATIONAL ENDOWMENT FOR THE HUMANITIES

Established by Congress in 1965 the Endowment for the Humanities is a grant making, independent agency charged to support research, education, preservation, and public programs in the humanities.

INSTITUTE OF MUSEUM AND LIBRARY SERVICES

Established by the 1996 National Foundation on the arts and Humanities by the Museum and Library Services Act (110Stat. 3009-293) which amended the Museum Service Act (20 U.S.C.961 et seq.) this office is charged with the programs formerly carried on within the Department of Education Museum and Library Services divisions and offices. This office is the nations primary support agency for 122,000 libraries and 17,000 museums. The mission is to create strong libraries and museums that connect people and ideas.

NATIONAL LABOR RELATIONS BOARD

The National Labor Relations Board is charged with the duty to safeguard private sector employees rights to organize and determine whether to have unions as their bargaining representatives. Established by the National Labor Relations Act of 1935 (Wagner Act 29 U.S.C. 167) this independent agency is authorized to assign appropriate units for collective bargaining.

NATIONAL MEDIATION BOARD

Established in 1934 by the National Railway Labor Act of 1926 (45 U.S.C.151-158) 160-162, 1181-1186) This board is charged with assigning units to facilitate harmonious labor relations in two major transportation industries, airlines and railways.

NATIONAL RAILROAD PASSENGER CORPORATION (AMTRAK)

Established by The Rail Passenger Service Act of 1970 (40 U.S.C 241) this office is charged with to provide balanced national rail service systems by developing, operating, and improving the U.S. Intercity rail passenger services. This will be discussed in later chapters.

NATIONAL SCIENCE FOUNDATION

Established by the National Science Foundation Act of 1950, as amended (42 U.S.C. 1861-1875) this Foundation is charged with he duty to increase the Nation's base of scientific and engineering knowledge and to develop and increase the science education of the nation.

NATIONAL TRANSPORTATION SAFETY BOARD

The 1974 Independent Safety Board Act (49 U.S.C. 1111) established this safety board to ensure that all types of transportation are conducted safely.

NUCLEAR REGULATORY COMMISSION

Established under the provisions of the Energy Reorganization Act of 1974 (42 U.S.C. 5801 et seq) and Executive Order 11834 in January 1975 this agency is an independent agency charged with ensuring safety of civilian nuclear use to protect the public health and safety as well as protect the environment. This agency was assigned the functions previously assigned to the Atomic Energy Commission. Added discussion on this aspect is included later in this book.

OCCUPATIONAL SAFETY AND HEALTH REVIEW COMMISSION

An independent quasi judicial commission to review and ensure timely and fair resolution of cases involving alleged exposure of American workers to unsafe or unhealthy working conditions. Established by the Occupational Safety and Health Act of 1970 (29 U.S.C. 651-678) the commission is in place to allow employers to dispute OSHA violation findings. Added discussion on this agency included in later chapters.

OFFICE OF THE DIRECTOR OF NATIONAL INTELLIGENCE

A Cabinet post level office created by section 1011 of the Intelligence and Reform and Terrorism Prevention Act of 2004 (50 U.S.C. 403) this office coordinates elements of the Intelligence Community and is the principal advisor to the President on Intelligence. Additional discussion of this agency will be in later chapters.

OFFICE OF THE GOVERNMENT ETHICS

Established under the Ethics in Government Act of 1978 (as amended, 5 U.S.C. app. 401) the Director of this Office is appointed by the President with the advice and consent of the President for a five year term. This office exercises leadership in the Executive Branch to prevent conflicts of interest of Government employees and to resolve conflicts of interest that do occur. Additional discussion of this agency will be in later chapters.

NOTE: July 27, 1917. This office appears to have been blindsided in the President's tweet on his decision to discriminate against transgender military personnel, and recruits. The President indicated he spoke to Generals and to military experts, he failed to discuss this with the Ethics in Government Office who might have reminded him that under the Ethics in Government ACT of Congress of 1978 (as amended, 56 U.S.C. app. 401) the government is not FREE to just change Constitutional rights on whimsy, or even demand of religious persons, or even generals. It will be interesting to see what the Ethics in Government lawyers have to say as they are bombarded by the Government employees who are already on media, and social media across the globe protesting the tweet. IF the comment that the military is not a social club, etc by the President were to be taken at ANY level equal treatment, he would have had to say that ANY military personnel, or recruit who cheats on their spouse, or has sex with prostitutes, or uses pornography must also be dismissed or refused to be allowed recruitment. Today's episode has shown an interesting reason for citizens READING and knowing the rights and functions of their governments. It would appear that an interesting debate and a LOT of law suits are going to result from the conflicts of interest of GENERALS and others who do not like gay persons, or trans-gendered persons could have been avoided if the President had asked the Office of Government Ethics if he might end up with a conflicts situation on separation of religion and state, and a slew of lawsuits against the government for discrimination. As he did not note if he was going to toss trans-gendered veterans, or VA staff workers or doctors out as well.......it will be interesting to see how that part of the issue unfolds. This is WHY these commissions and advisors are in place, to keep our government out of such issues that will further divide the citizens, and cost the taxpayers a LOT of money.

OFFICE OF PERSONNEL MANAGEMENT

Established by the Reorganization Plan No. 2 of 1978 (5 U.S.C. app) this office administers a merit system to ensure compliance with personnel laws and regulations and to assist agencies in recruiting, examining and promoting people with the necessary skills and experience rather than those without these requisites to Federal employment.

OFFICE OF SPECIAL COUNSEL

Established January 1, 1979 by Reorganization Act No. 2 of 1978 (5 U.S.C. 1101) The Civil Service Act of 1978 (4 U.S.C. 1101 note) which became effective January 11, 1979 enlarging its powers pursuant to the provisions of the Whistleblower Protection Act of 1989 (5 U.S.C. 1211 et seq) charged with the litigation of the Merit Systems Protection Board.

OVERSEAS PRIVATE INVESTMENT CORPORATION

Established in 1971 by the Foreign Affairs and Reform and Restructuring Act (112 stat. 2681-790) as a self sustaining Federal Agency that is charged with promoting economic growth in developing countries and emerging markets by encouraging

American investment in those nations. Additional comments on this agency are in another chapter.

PEACE CORPS

Established by the Peace Corps Act of 1961 as amended (22 U.S.C. 2501) Peace Corps is charged to help people in interested countries in meeting their need for trained men and women, and to promote better understanding between America and other countries.

PENSION BENEFIT GUARANTY CORPORATION

A self financing agency subject to the Government Corporation Control Act (31 U.S>C. 9101, 9109), the Title IV provisions of the Employee Retirement income Security Act of 1974 (29 U.S.C.1301-1461) this office is charged with protecting the pension benefits of private sector employees. Additional comments on this agency are in another chapter.

POSTAL REGULATORY COMMISSION

This is the successor Commission to the Postal Rate Commission created by the Postal Reorganization Act as amended (39 U.S.C. 301-3604. The Commission became an independent agency in the Postal Accountability act (39 U.S.C.101 note). Five commissioners are appointed by the President, with advice and consent of the Senate, one commissioner is designated as Chairman.

The duties of the commission are to develop and implement a modern system of postal regulation.

RAILROAD RETIREMENT BOARD

Established by the Railroad Retirement Act of 1944 (as amended (45 U.S.C. 201-228z-1) this agency administers comprehensive retirement survivor, and unemployment, sickness benefit programs for railroad workers and their families.

SECURITIES AND EXCHANGE COMMISSION

Established by the Securities and Exchange Act of 1934 (15 U.S.C. 78-1-78-jj)this commission serves as advisor to the US District Courts in connection with reorganization proceedings for debtor corporations and administers cases where there is considerable public interest. This commission also sets the policies and administrates their registration statements to ensure public offerings are fully and fairly disclosed to the public.

SELECTIVE SERVICES SYSTEM

Established by the Military Selective Service Act, (50 U.S.C. app. 451-471a) this agency oversees the registration and keeps track of all males over the age of 18 who are required by law to register with Selective Service. At present there is no draft due to a public demand after the War in Vietnam to discontinue the draft.

Although there is no draft, males, and in some cases women of qualitative age are required to register with Selective Service.

This is an example of the PEOPLE backing down before an issue was completed. In a recent documentary on PBS past DOD Secretary Rumsfeld discussed the draft and the reality that with so few soldiers volunteering and being involved in war that the PEOPLE just do not care what the military does. THAT is a sad truth for Americans, when they ALL were at risk, they cared, now they are not involved, so they do not care about the military or the veterans. The President has recently exposed from talking to combat soldiers the lacks and problems that have gone without care, by Congress, or the public for many years. The recent VA Bill is an indication that the Congress and President are beginning to look at those problems and create change. Examples noted in media this week included the removal from Student Loans for veterans of schools and technical programs that went out of business before giving them their certificates or degrees, and allowing them new opportunities to find an approved resource to get that education or technical certificate so they can get sustainable employment. Hopefully this trend will continue.

SMALL BUSINESS ADMINISTRATION

Established by the Small Business Act of 1953 this agency is given the duty to aid, counsel, assist and protect the interests of small businesses. The web site, and materials in all the regional offices of the SBA encourage citizens to consider private small business, and provide trainings and assistance to meet their end goals.

SOCIAL SECURITY ADMINISTRATION

Established by the Social Security Administration and Reorganization Plan No. 2 of 1946 (5 U.S.C. app) became effective July 16, 1946 to manage the nation's social security benefit system and to protect the workplace enforced mandatory deductions which every private sector employee is expected to have removed from their pay checks, and is monitored to ensure the employers make the appropriate deposits to the Social Security Administration benefits fund. The Social Security Administration also administrates the Social Security Disability programs and dependants programs.

TENNESSEE VALLEY AUTHORITY

This is a special agency that controls and administrates the Flood Control area including navigation, electric power plant productions and transmission recreation improvement, water supply, water quality, environmental and economic development.

TRADE AND DEVELOPMENT AGENCY

Established by Act in 1980, The trade and Development agency is charged with advance economic and US commercial interests in developing countries. There is additional discussion of this agency in other chapters.

UNITED STATES AGENCY FOR INTERNATIONAL DEVELOPMENT

Established by the Foreign Assistance Act of 1961 (22 U.S.C. 6563) this agency administers the United States foreign economic and humanitarian assistance programs worldwide as directed by the Secretary of State.

UNITED STATES COMMISSION ON CIVIL RIGHTS

Established by the Civil Rights Act of 1957 as amended and re-established by the United States Commission on Civil Rights Act of 1994 as amended (42 U.S.C. 1975) This agency is charged with the collection, research, studies of information on discrimination or denials of equal protection laws for race, color, religion, sex, age, disability, national origin or in the administration of justice to such areas as voting rights, equal opportunity in education, employment and housing, and Federal Civil rights laws being upheld.

UNITED STATES INTERNATIONAL TRADE COMMISSION

Created by the Revenue Act (39 Stat. 795) originally named the United States Tariff Commission, this office is charged with furnishing studies papers, reports, and recommendations involving international trade, and tariffs to the President, The US Trade Representative and Congressional Committees. This office also investigates numerous types of complaints related to International Trade.

UNITED STATES POSTAL SERVICE

Established as an independent agent, by the executive branch in the Postal Reorganization act (39 U.S.C. 101 et seq) the present Postal Service July 1, 1971. Charg with processing mail, and delivery services to persons and businesses across the nation the Postal Service has a long history of methods. The Postal Service has its own research and development programs to increase service and efficiency, and a Postal investigation service to investigate complaints and crimes that violate postal laws.

QUASI OFFICIAL AGENCIES

The agencies listed in this category are agencies that are not parts of the Federal Government, but are related to public service and may be funded, or partially funded by Federal grants, and/or appropriations of Congress. Each year the listings in this area are changed due to adding new offices, or old offices closing or becoming part of a government department.

The web sites of these quasi official agencies provides the most current information on their standing and operations.

LEGAL SERVICES CORPORATION

SMITHSONIAN INSTITUTION

STATE JUSTICE INSTITUTE

UNITED STATES INSTITUTE OF PEACE

EACH ONE of these bureaus, agencies, and departments has web sites, and information available to those who are interested in the subject matter. Those programs such as art, science, the humanities, libraries all have contact information for local areas across the nation to increase and interest people in their subject matter.

Note: EVERY agency has an Inspector General with whom complaints and concerns may be filed. These oversight agency additions may be within the Agency itself, or with a governing agency. The observation was made by several persons during the informal preliminary surveys that these offices often tell complainants that they can not reveal what happens with the complaint, and that complaints are considered and acted upon as research suggests applicable. The personal thought of the author is that our current President in one of his books on business stated that if the leadership is overwhelmed with "putting out fires" that administration is not doing its job properly and needs to reassess and correct the organization until the complaints are either few, or none........if any citizen were to contact their own local representative, the staff would tell them the complaints are overwhelming. It appears to the author that this allegation would be an impetus for getting in and doing the work needed to resolve the issues, not hire more staff to send out "we get too many emails to reply personally" or "thanks for the thoughts" letters and emails to their constituents. I have volunteered for elected politicians to open and assess mail, and that had been a job I had during college at a large bank. The reply the constituents WANT is to see their problems resolved, not a personalized form letter or email saying thanks for the thoughts.

THE REASSESSMENT AND RESTRUCTURING OF PUBLIC AGENCIES

Obviously there are many reasons to reassess and restructure any business. The study of Public Administration deals with the administration of the business of day to day implementation of the mandates of each agency or department. Unlike a regular, money making business, where a product or service is sold and MUST be evaluated periodically to assure the product or service is still viable as a business profit making unit for sale, in a government agency or department the sole assessment needs to be: IS THE agency or department meeting the mandate that created the agency or department No agency or department of the Federal government can exist without Federal funding. This creates many levels of safeguards for the taxpayers money to be protected from waste, embezzlement, or misuse.

However, it has in reality, also provided many levels to hide bad deeds, embezzlement and misuse of funds which need to be examined and eliminated. The General Accounting Office (GEO) has the mandated task of making sure there are adequate oversights and programs to disallow abuse, waste, and embezzling of taxpayer funds. The reassessing of public agencies and departments needs to be done each year, the above branches each have adequate research groups and policy advisory groups to protect the taxpayers from being defrauded. The problem appears to be one of making it plain and simple to ALL government employees, which orientation and oaths are expected to do, that their only employer is the PEOPLE of the United States of America and their allegiance is to the Constitution and the laws, NOT to their supervisor, or a lobbyist, Congressperson, or party manipulator of which the system is apparently as filled as it is with lobbyists.

If, as an example, a private business had the stated business of making chairs, and the employer came in and asked "what are you doing?" and the employee answered "building a doll house for my cousin's little girl", it would be expected the employee would be charged with stealing from the company and fired. Yet daily our agencies and departments do NOT do the job that is plainly and clearly mandated for them. They would rather spend three or four million dollars on a survey and study, which just fortunately their husband, wife, cousin, useless daughter or son, or even more useless niece or nephew, mistress or boyfriend happens to have a company that performs that type of survey or study, rather than to DO the job the enabling legislation requires.

How dare we as a country spend millions of dollars across the nation doing studies to see if the American children and teens are getting a good all around education to prepare them for life and self sustainability when we only have to glance around anywhere at random to see we are not providing large numbers with the skills and opportunities to be self sustaining. We do not need a study, or that study could be the administrator walking through town for just ONE day during work and/or school hours and noting what the children and youth are doing. I personally have gone out to the park, or fast food restaurants, or taken a ride on the bus during school hours, and found upon discussion with the youth that are ALL truant, that they do NOT have the education or skills to be self sustaining, AND the majority of them comment that NO ONE cares. I was volunteering at a school where a young person wrote on his journal page after I had assured him he was free to write anything he wanted to or felt: The teachers just yell at the bad kids, and we don't learn anything, and NO ONE CARES". I sent a copy of that page to President G. W. Bush, he initiated No Child Left Behind, which would seem to be a very clear message, but, by the time it got down to classrooms, it was the "bad" kids being shuffled to rooms in the Ed Center where they did NOTHING! Many of the youth I surveyed in that room ended up in lock down programs I volunteered for, and did very well, they just needed proper teachers and support.

Take a look at ANY news program and see what our youth and teens are doing, bullying a disabled man while he drowns, driving the wrong way on the freeway and taking selfies of oneself getting into an accident, harming the homeless, robbing or raping senior citizens, molesting and assaulting other youth and teens. Saying "where you from" and shooting anyone who is not from wherever it is the shooters want that person to be from. Has any city done a count, NOT a study, of how many soldiers survived the war and came home and were shot in gangland "where you from" drive by shootings? In our city there are at least three, and it is an upper income urban city, NOT a ghetto or gang infested neighborhood.

These are NOT the acts of people with an adequate education and upbringing. Whether the youth, their parents, or society, or the schools, WELL PAID to educate and help them find POSITIVE life goals, SOMEONE is to blame for this, and we do NOT need more million dollar studies to tell us it is a problem. We do NOT need more slick books and folders for conferences on "oh dear me, what can we do?" and then do NOTHING.

Reassessing and restructuring public agencies is looking at the enabling legislation and making sure the money allocated is being used to its best penny to do what the legislation was put in place for. It means making sure that when the Department of Housing gets another billion to get the homeless homed, that foreign landlords to NOT buy more property and raise the rents to get that money. These realities are what created the need for this study. In this area, I requested a graduate level class I was attending to do its weekly paper about what COULD we do to END homelessness. One of the suggestions, from the class, as well as HUD and other government home supportive agency staff informal surveys , was to have a Federal Rent Control. It was a simple addition to IRS and HUD, with a fast implementation. Pass the Bill, and give thirty days for compliance, then every land owner out of compliance could no longer collect rent. The follow up paper was to informally survey rental companies for input. Most of them saw the positive aspects, and suggested how to reduce paperwork. The compliance was just an IRS rent tax code. NO ONE would have to pay rent to a landlord without that code, and those checks HAD to be deposited in banks that would report the funds to IRS and State Tax Boards.

No one would be able to obtain that IRS tax number without a State landlord ID number, and that could not be obtained without a local code enforcement and business license clearance. ONE home, rented to FAMILY members could be exempted. The formal business realty companies and rental management companies said that local code enforcement clearance would give their clients support, because the pictures and reports would show the property WAS in good condition when rented. The informal surveys of renters felt exactly the same, they would no longer be along and on their own to try and enforce what code enforcement told them was legal......they would NOT have to pay rent on property not properly cleared by local code enforcement, AND they would have pictures and proof that they had NOT destroyed the property when code enforcement came to reassess the property for the next rental. These standards could easily be locally generated and enforced.

The inability to collect rent on slum lands and housing would raise the standard of living of ALL areas of the United States, and would put more property on the market.

Note: while researching this area, many cases were in the papers of slum landlords and the inability of even code enforcement and the cities to get them to make the buildings safe, and lawful.

The enforced tax on ALL rents would also discourage the foreign slum landlords, since they would have to have a formal IRS filing number that included their income information. It was just a fluke, but one day while going in to Social Security I was sitting at a desk waiting for the worker, when I overheard the worker talking to the lady next to me. She kept trying to tell him that she did not owe tax on her income properties because she collected the rents in cash, and sent the cash to other countries where it was used to buy more property for her company (I wondered if it was also slum property, which had become clear it was considered here in America as she tried to talk the man into exempting the amount of the legal fees for slum landlord lawsuits from her "income" to be taxed.)

There was another case in the papers about a slum landlord that the judge got so frustrated with he sentenced the man to live in one of his own slum apartment buildings, with a band on his leg and not able to leave his house arrest. The news of course showed the horrible conditions in that building, with rats, falling down conditions, and bugs, as well as trash all over the halls and yards, and some very unsavory tenants that the neighbors and POLICE had been complaining about for months.

REASSESSING PUBLIC AGENCIES

In beginning PhD level Public Administration courses, the student learns to do the annual mandatory evaluations of the agency. In a private business the business has a very important self interest in making sure these assessments are true and complete. If a business creates a survey that shows "everyone" wants our product, when in fact no one wants that product or service, the business will fail based on spending money on products and service workers costs with no income. Yet, many a public administration administrator has told me that in reality, the agency proves it spent every penny of their past year allocations and needs more, no matter how they wasted the money, or if the actual need for the agency even exists anymore, or if there is ANY correlation between how much is spent and how many are actually benefiting from the money the taxpayers are FORCED to give for the budget. NO business could succeed being run in that way.

RESTRUCTURING PUBLIC AGENCIES

In a private business, based upon the surveys and observations of the employees and department leadership, changes are evaluated by projections and studies to ensure the business is not going to fail because of the restructuring or the failure to restructure. A private business that perhaps makes bottles to contain private label jelly and jam might review their sales to decide if the business is still viable in financial return to pay all expenses and make enough of a financial profit to be worth continuing the same sales products.

By comparison, if a government agency is mandated to perform a specific service under the mandates that created it, and there no longer are any persons in need of that service, the agency might be considered for closure, or being combined into another similar agency, should the need once again arise for the service covered in the mandates. In addition, all the policy change projections and advisories are by law required to be submitted to the appropriate oversight branches of government and if created by an Act of Congress, to Congress to be changed or eliminated. All of these procedures are required to be public, with public notice to allow the voters to communicate their views to their Congresspersons on the proposed Act to change government.

Two major issues arise in public agency restructuring that create differences between a business, and an agency in need of reassessment and restructuring. Those issues are that a business is not mandated by Congress to request a reassessment process and a business is not mandated by Congress to implement changes suggested following the restructuring design being created. This has led to two major slowing areas in reassessing public agencies and then restructuring them if needed. A business completes an annual, or semi-annual process to evaluate itself for profit to keep from failing. A business can call a meeting, create a process to reassess, and meet again to discuss the issues in the over sight reassessment.

This might occur within the period of a few hours as there do not appear to be legal mandates to fulfill requiring permissions from Congress. A public agency on the other hand has been give the strange task of preparing the supportive documentation that it needs reassessment, while not having been given the funds or the authority to do so. This works in the favor of any agency or government department that does NOT want its inner workings made public, they just claim they can not afford to do the paperwork necessary to find out what is needed. The taxpayers need to demand that this be remedied fast and efficiently for every agency and department of the government, whether city, county, state of Federal government agencies.

Oversight: One of the areas that could definitely be researched for a new study would be the types of oversight reports due, and the mandates on their compliance. While the boxes of paper sent to me by agency administrators, and the web sites filled with rules and regulations concerning oversight were extensive, the simple questions, such as IS the agency doing what the enabling legislation created it to do, and IS that being done in an efficient manner, and WHERE is all that money going, are NOT answered.

The following section contains workbooks of materials we use in our programs based on the Constitution and the Ten Rights and Responsibilities of ALL Humans that were utilized in the UNA/ USA and foreign teaching programs for many years.

They are entered here to show how much can be done at no expense at all. ALL of the materials are contained in the Constitution and the Constitution of the United Nations.

These are educational programs for our high risk and veterans and their families programs.

The equine therapy programs are used by our high risk youth and veterans programs as animal assisted therapy programs. While there are many psychiatric programs using horses as couches, there are also many VETSRIDEFREE and OPERATION FREE RIDE programs across the nation where individual horse owners, and small stables and community programs use the riding and exhibition shows for fundraising at their own cost, or paid through fundraising and/or grant and donations from the community.

THE TEN RIGHTS AND RESPONSIBILITIES OF EVERY HUMAN ON EARTH

The Ten Rights and Responsibilities of every human being on earth was a learning lesson for the children and adults in the United Nations UNICEF programs. Many cities around the country had UNA/USA gift shops and a classroom where public and private schools, religious groups and community programs came to learn about the United Nations and the rights and responsibilities we each have to make this a world that expands the vision of the Founders of The United States of America to be a global concept.

This portion of this book is from a workbook we developed for our UNA/USA students from the Declarations of the United Nations since we could not find the old materials, and could only remember nine of the rights we used to teach. Using the Constitution of the United Nations, we developed our own ten rights, with apologies to the original list which we could not find anywhere.

A WORKBOOK/ TEN RIGHTS & TEN RESPONSIBLITIES
Of EVERY HUMAN

INTRODUCTION

The United Nations was a vision of First Lady Eleanor Roosevelt. She was the wife of President Roosevelt who was working to bring America out of a depression that made millions of Americans homeless, and without proper food, clothing, shelter, or jobs.

The United Nations sought to bring the rights of the Constitution to International levels, and make sure every person was given the rights Americans believe are the rights of everyone.

In classes taught to school children across America, and in other nations, the United Nations started to teach all humans that if we expect rights for ourselves, we need to take on the duty to make sure all other humans get those same rights. These were the UN/ USA teaching programs Ten Rights and Ten Responsibilities.

The original training paperwork has been lost. Years of searching and asking various departments of the United Nations for help, has turned up nothing. The authors remembered most of the Rights and Responsibilities. The United Nations Declarations contain the material to match up the rights. The authors have created a work book for children and youths, to be translated into as many languages as possible to work towards asking children around the world to help Eleanor's Dream come true. Eleanor Roosevelt had a dream of children around the world growing into a new global international relationship of many governments, and many cultures. A place where all the world's people would be safe to learn about one another, and to respect the right of others to be different than themselves. Eleanor Roosevelt had a great dream, one that would take the commitment of all the world's people to make it come true.

The authors have created this workbook for teachers, and parents to work along with their children to build their own skills in global relationships that will lead to a world at peace with plenty for all of us, and a dedicated global citizenry that protects and enjoys all of the animals, plants, and gifts of nature, and preserves them for the generations to come. Each of the ten rights and responsibilities has exercises to be done in classrooms, and at home, or in children's programs.

UNICEF has in the past been a fundraising and education program for the health of the world's children. The orange boxes at Halloween were well known. The children took them out Trick or Treating. The adults had a cache of pennies, nickels and dimes to put in the boxes for children who brought them to the door. Along with candy and treats, the children learned to be heroes in the world. Often just two or three pennies gave a packet of minerals or went towards the cost of vaccinations for children all over the world. Many times, just a few pennies saved a life.

Classrooms, and youth groups took the boxes and passed them to each student from time to time to take home and fill, or NOT, Schools and cities often created awards ceremonies, and classroom parties to reward those who raised the largest amounts of money. While it was amazing when some private schools raised large amounts of money, the awards were based on more than just money, poster, tee shirt design and other program ideas by the youth themselves factored in to the awards. How did they raise the money? Private schools were in a class by themselves so as not to be in direct competition with children and families without access to the large amounts of money.

The authors have created this workbook in hopes children and parents will once again take up the fun and the personal heroism of helping others. As the global community grows closer due to mass/fast transportation and the internet, the authors hope the world's children and their parents will become the building blocks of an international community that will be there for each other when natural, or health crisis occurs.

Ten Rights and Responsibilities of Every Human

1. The Right to Clean Air
2. The Right to Clean Water
3. The Right to nutritious and adequate food
4. The Right to warm and healthy shelter
5. The Right to life: healthcare, nutrition, safety
6. The Right to liberty: Justice, no slavery
7. The Right to the pursuit of happiness: education for the joy of learning
8. The Right to a good job: education and State reform for jobs
9. The Right to belong: no non-country persons
10. The Right to belong: freedom of religion, freedom of membership, freedom of assembly, no racism, no gender bias

Ten Responsibilities

1. The Responsibility to keep the Air Clean
2. The Responsibility to keep the Water Clean
3. The Responsibility to make sure there is nutritious and adequate food for everyone
4. The Responsibility to make sure there is warm and healthy shelter for everyone
5. The Responsibility to make sure there is healthcare, nutrition and safety for everyone
6. The Responsibility to make sure there is freedom, justice, no slavery so everyone can be free
7. The Responsibility to make sure everyone has a good education for the joy of learning and to make sure they can pursue their dreams
8. The Responsibility to make sure that education and every State and Nation has reforms to give jobs to everyone who wants one, including the disabled, young, and elderly
9. The Responsibility to make sure that no one is made homeless, without a country
10. The Responsibility to make sure that everyone has freedom to belong to groups as they see fit, as long as they are not harming others (these include freedom of religion, and political party membership without armed or violent attempts to overtake governments (philosophy, not violence).

THE RIGHT TO CLEAN AIR/THE RESPONSIBILITY TO KEEP THE AIR CLEAN

People need clean air.

Plants, animals, even rain and the earth's atmosphere are changed by changes in the air.

Breathe deeply.

Is the air you are breathing clean and healthy?

What does clean air look like?

Draw a picture of clean air.

Draw a picture of dirty air.

What are some causes of dirty air?

How can each of us make sure that the causes of dirty air are remedied?

One of the biggest causes of dirty air is human industrial burning and air borne waste.

If we were to help companies clean up their mess, and find research to help them keep costs down while still providing their products and services, how do you see that happening?

What could each of us do to help companies and legislators make this a reality? In our cities, counties, States and Nations?

THE RIGHT TO CLEAN WATER/THE RESPONSIBILITY FOR CLEAN WATER

Everyone needs clean water.

Look into the internet resources and see how many people are not getting clean water.

Look on the internet and see how many people are really helping others get clean water, and how many are just using it as a scam.

How do we tell the difference between those who really use our money and volunteer hours to help others, and those who just scam our money by pretending to care about others.

What do you do with water every day?

Draw pictures of some of the things you use water for.

How would it feel to brush your teeth with water from the toilet bowl?

How about getting a drink of water out of the bath tub after the family have all taken a bath?

Did you know that many people all over the world use small streams and creeks, ponds, and rivers to bathe, do laundry, and wash dishes in? Think of some ways to keep cultural traditions, but still have clean water?

How can we educate people that two or three people bathing or washing dishes and clothes in the river is not the same as a hundred, or a thousand, or more?

How can we help to make sure clean water to drink and use for health reasons is available to everyone?

How can we all save water so there is enough for everyone, everyday?

What kind of jobs are related to water?

How are scientists working to help make water use better?

Years of putting garbage, and toxic waste in the dirt has caused the dirt itself to dirty water. What can we do to help clean the dirt?

How can we get companies to come forward and ask for help to clean up toxic water and dirt problems without fearing they will be sued or put in jail?

Which is more important? Punishing people or companies, or getting the whole earth clean for dirt and water?

President Jimmy Carter suggested we have wars to end poverty. Maybe we need to encourage companies that make war products to turn their thought to a new kind of war. What kind of products would the world need to make sure the water and dirt of the world are clean? What kind of products are used for war, that could be turned to products for peace so the employees will not lose their jobs?

Did you know that President George W. Bush equipped many of our air craft carriers to be immediately helpful in major world disasters? What other ways can we use our "swords" as "plowshares" and let our military be prepared, but also help in peacetime disasters?

Presidents Jimmy Carter, Bill Clinton, Bush (father and son), and Obama, now President Trump will also have spent time making trips and working with world leaders to create peace on the earth. What would you suggest to them as they continue to work together (even if they are from different political parties, and backgrounds) to help companies that make money on war to begin to help the world change and make money on peace, and on the suggested wars on poverty?

Like police, military will probably always be necessary in the world, but like police, could this become a trained and ready group to help humans, rather than war, war, war?

What can your parents do to help the world get along better?

What can you do to help the world get along better?

More on this subject is discussed in other rights and responsibilities.

There are projects that clean the oceans, rivers, and streams. Look in the internet and list some of them. What if each of these projects had as much money as war to pay people to clean up the water and all the places that are dirtying water? Write some jobs you can think of all over the world to make sure water is clean.

Some of the jobs are going to be hard work. Maybe instead of student loans, young healthy people could do those jobs for shorter hours or for college breaks and earn the money for college instead of mounting up debt. Think of some other people who might do the hard work.

Think of ways the hard work could be fun.

Water needs pipes and workers to get to where people need it. Sometimes hurricanes, tsunami, and tornados and earthquakes destroy the pipes or cause too much water at one time. Think of some ways we could have special funds for emergencies so that everyone has water, and that water emergencies are taken care of immediately.

What kind of jobs would this create?

Sometimes there are droughts and times when there is not enough water?

What can we do to make sure we have systems ready to make sure water is available so people, animals and plants have adequate water?

What kind of jobs would this create worldwide?

Some people think animals should just do without water....they do not realize that humans have made dams, and use more water than they used to for big cities and agriculture, and by putting freeways and cities in the way of animals migrating to places with more water and food part of the year.

How can humans develop water and food resources for animals that are starving or doing without water because of human reasons?

THE RIGHT TO NUTRITIOUS AND ADEQUATE FOOD/RESPONSIBILTY TO MAKE SURE EVERYONE HAS NUTRITIOUS AND ADEQUATE FOOD

Explore the internet.

What are the two sides of this issue?

The Right to Nutritious and adequate food is one that the original United Nations founders felt was necessary for every human.

Think about the problems this causes for the major kinds of economies in the world.

In certain cultures, the old, the disabled, those who do not have enough, are just left to die. How does your country meet the needs of the old, the disabled?

In other cultures, the rich are often jailed, and in ancient times were killed or exiled if they did not make sure the least had everything they needed.

Look at your own country. What are the government standards for feeding people?

Does this agree with the principles of the United Nations vision?
How can we help others without disrespecting their culture?

How do we keep dishonest people from raising the price of food if they know the government is going to pay for food for everyone?

How can each of us help to make sure everyone has nutritious and adequate food without costing the taxpayers more money than it should cost?

In America there are many people who feel the cost of feeding others is not their job?

What do you think?

How do you think each State can keep the costs under control?

How can each County keep the costs under control?

How can each family make sure they create their own nutritious and adequate food supply?

In old times parents often told their children to clean their plate, to think of the children starving somewhere else.

Today, while children and others starve in some places, many people throw away food.

How could we get people to not take so much food, and not waste it.

Can you find programs that help people to grow their own food?

How could your class or your family raise money to help one family grow their own food?

How could we suggest and get cooperation from our food companies to donate more food to areas that need it, or to fund small stores in those areas where the food could be sold for less?

Would your family pay one penny more for every can, bottle, or box of food you buy if the companies would pledge to take all those pennies and send food at low cost to small stores that would sell it and help employ and feed areas that are needing help until they are on their feet, and able to help others?

Would your family pay one penny more for every can, bottle or box of food you buy if the companies would build some of their big super stores in areas that really, really need them, but would have to have the items at a discounted price from what we in many countries can afford?

There are corporations and small companies that already try to do this, what could your class or family do to help them build the idea until their job is easier, and they can give more to those who need it until they are part of the giving and no longer need the help?

Can you find some groups, companies and corporations that help out the world food programs?

How can you find out if they are real, or if they are just raising money for themselves, using poor people and needy people as a way to get people to donate?

How can we, as a world, make it harder for people to steal from donations for the poor and those in disaster areas?

THE RIGHT TO WARM AND HEALTHY SHELTER/RESPONSIBILITY TO MAKE SURE EVERYONE HAS WARM AND HEALTHY SHELTER

The right to warm and healthy shelter

What does this mean?

Think of all the types of housing there are.

Should this mean that everyone has to live in the same kind of house as everyone else?

Who are all the people in our society that are important to people have a home that is warm and healthy?

How do other societies differ?

Should a person be allowed to be "homeless"?

What does this mean?

Is it OK for us to let a person who wants a home, but is old, ill, or disabled, or young live in the street?

Who should pay for helping the homeless have homes?

Who pays for these things in other countries?

There are systems called "economic systems" look these up and learn about them. People have disagreed about these systems for many reasons. Compare the systems to our systems of today. What do you think? Are they really that different?

Thomas Jefferson had strong ideas about the way the economy for America needed to be guided. He had a vision of everyone living in communities that in my mind are like mainstreet at Disneyland, or Disneyworld. You could buy things and get services you needed, but everyone had homes where they could sustain their own families as well. The study of President Jefferson and his ideas, and those who opposed him are very important when learning about world economy and how we all have responsibility to make sure that the principles of the Constitution are fulfilled, at least in our own country and those we support by buying products and selling products (import and export) and allowing Americans to travel to those countries.

Write about how you would see changes in your own city to make it better for those who are sick, old, or too poor to have a home.

What is your city doing to help the homelessness problems in America?

Think about your family. What if they had a huge hurricane, or other natural disaster and your own family needed help beyond what their home insurance would pay. What could your family do to help build a better system of family responsibility? What could your community do to help? What could the whole country do to make sure in major disaster everyone gets back to at least basic shelter, water, and food as soon as possible?

The Right to life: healthcare, nutrition, safety/ the Responsibility to make sure others have healthcare, nutrition and safety.

The Right to Life. The Constitution of the United States gives every single person the right to life, liberty and the pursuit of happiness. Learn about these rights so you can understand the United Nations concept for life, liberty and freedom to be yourself in peace and happiness.

What can we each do to make sure everyone has these basic needs met?

In the United Nations, the countries are asked to make commitments to the same basic rights for all humans.

Not all countries belong to the United Nations.

Not all countries are doing their best to make these principles of the founders of the United Nations, or the legislators who put together the Constitution and the Manual of The United States Government are being upheld.

What can each of us do to make sure that these principles are met worldwide?

The Right to liberty: Justice, no slavery
The Responsibility to see everyone has liberty, justice and no slavery.

Everyone has the right to liberty. What does this mean?

Look up the Constitution of the United States. What do discussions of liberty mean when related to the United States?

How does this relate to the liberty of all people in the United Nations?

How can Americans make sure that other people have liberty?

What do you think of justice today. Look into the Constitution and the rights that are guaranteed. Do you think these rights are being protected for everyone in America?

What can a single person do to make sure others have justice?

The right to not be enslaved is one guaranteed in the United States of America. Look at the Amendments to the Constitution. Read the discussions and arguments of the Founders of the Constitution. Why do you think some of them wanted slavery?

Slavery is in many countries, including America today. America is supposed to be rooting it out and prosecuting people. Can you find examples of this in the news?

If a person has to work too many hours, and cannot enjoy his/her life, and can not afford to pay for a home, food, clothes, education for their family, is it a kind of slavery?

Do mandatory costs that cause prices to soar create a kind of slavery for the working middle class?

What can be done to make sure people work, but not in bad conditions, and for too little money to live on.

What can you do to help make sure slavery is not a part of the products that you use, or the companies that you buy services from?

The Right to the pursuit of happiness: education for the joy of learning
The Responsibility to see others all have the freedom to pursue happiness and
Education that gives them the joy of learning and the ability to work

The pursuit of happiness means that every person should have time to find his or her own dream and work on making it come true. To have their family, buy a home if they want to, to have savings, and time for vacations and to see family members when they are celebrating weddings, anniversaries, birthdays, and other holidays, as well as when people are sick, or to go for family funerals, or memorials.

Happiness, is not always happy. But to be free to have time off work without fear of being fired to care for a dying relative is a form of happiness.

What are other forms of happiness people should have time and money to pursue?

Education is a form of happiness. Each time you read a book, or learn a lesson from a video, or class, you are sharing with a person you do not know. Hopefully that person loved what they wrote about and wanted to teach about.

Education should be a joy. Some things in education are hard, and take time to learn, but the pursuit of that education should still be a joy.

What can you do to make sure you get your education?

What can you do to make sure others get their education?

The Right to a good job: education and State reform for jobs
The Responsibility to make sure others have a good job opportunity, the education
to get the jobs, and that their State or Nation has reforms to protect both jobs and
those who are employed in many ways

If you are given a free education, what can you do to make the most of it?

Because it is free, do you have to take it or leave it, or do you have a right to ask for what YOU need to get a good job, to learn how to read and use technology to grow your own life.

The Right to belong: no non-country persons
The Right to belong: freedom of religion, freedom of membership,
freedom of assembly

Can you find examples of people who do NOT have a place to belong?

What can we all do to make sure this is changed for everyone?

CLOSING THOUGHTS:

"See opportunity where others see only obstacles" ....TD Jakes

A police chief once remarked that his vision would be a city that could return to Mayberry. A city where people were educated, and inspired to be good citizens, where the police were support, service, protection no more cops and robbers. His dream: the ability to know the "bad guys" and be able to talk them out of crime, rather than have to play cops and robbers. His thoughts made me think about the story of Mayberry, where Barney, talking to and knowing all the people was a greater deterrent to crime than more and more militarized police departments separated from the people. The duty to resolve the problems in our country are BOTH the police and the citizens of every CITY. To work together and find resolution, not compromise, or "make" anyone do anything.

Reading through the Constitution, the Ten Rights and Responsibilities of the United Nations, and the Manual of the United States Government one thing is clear, many others have had the vision to create a country and world where humans were a plus, not just a game of Monopoly or cops and robbers where a tiny number took over the resources, and the earth, animals and humans suffered. The missions of agencies were meant to guide the use of taxpayer money for the support of taxpayers and others should they ever need help. Some of the legislation appears almost whimsical and out of sync with the reality of the agencies being run under the guise of meeting the enabling legislative goals.

Oversight on almost every agency is clearly not working. For example, If we see a homeless person, housing is NOT doing its job. There is not one word in the legislation that says spend hundreds of millions on the surveys regarding homelessness. While knowing WHY people are homeless may help know what kinds of housing to facilitate to end the problems of homelessness, counting the homeless year after year seems pointless and a waste of money. The police can easily tell you a fair and similar estimate of the numbers of homeless at no extra expense. If there were tiered programs for homelessness (this has been piloted in Las Vegas and worked) where the police bring in persons and if they can not prove they have homes to be redirected to, there are mandatory programs that help identify the why of homelessness while helping the person gain goals and help to become housed once again. NO wasted paperwork. Just help and the people are off the street, getting help.

People are dying from lack of healthcare. Since 1993, when President Clinton began to talk about healthcare, Congress has known that one of the leading causes of death in America was lack of healthcare. Insurance, healthcare denied by insurance companies who had been paid, and just plain malpractice are major causes of death of Americans, yet with all our surveys and research, we have not one study that shows the real numbers of how many Americans have died since 1980 when healthcare changed from health CARE to mandatory insurance. Twenty years after the conversation opened in CONGRESS with the 1993 mandatory insurance legislation was defeated we are no closer to closing the gap and no one has any idea of how many thousands each year have died from the lack of appropriate healthcare since insurance companies and for profit companies put the charitable hospitals and private doctor run hospitals and clinics out of business. Even though we now have mandatory insurance, it is doing no better, the stories of those who are suffering, with plenty of insurance, but NO CARE are growing each day. CONGRESS persons on CSPAN covered hearings are beginning to discuss this reality of mandatory insurance.

The President of the United States is given the absolute burden to make sure no person on our lands is impoverished (The Manual of The United States Government, 2004), or to suffer the effects of poverty. Those effects are listed as homelessness, lack of medical care, lack of proper nutrition, and lack of proper care for the disabled, seniors and young. President Roosevelt added those provisions with his supporting Congress to make sure that at least one of the Executive Branches of the United States was responsible for the living conditions of the PEOPLE. His thought seemed to be that if he made the President responsible for what are now the Ten Rights and Ten Responsibilities of ALL humans under the provisions of the United Nations.......that President could be impeached for not keeping those duties fulfilled.

There laws were enacted by President Roosevelt and Congress to ensure another depression would never occur. When President Reagan was sued on this duty as he attempted to take Social Security benefits and give them to other agencies, the Court agreed, and the Presidential lawyers agreed to leave Social Security alone if the suit was not pursued. This duty was still in the older copies of the Manual of the United States Government, but had disappeared by the 2008 printing. NOTHING can be removed from the legislation held in the manual without an ACT of CONGRESS, which must be done publicly. There are many other instances of laws just being ejected, or changed in the later Manuals. After the death of Roosevelt passed away, there are agencies added without proper Act to establish their mandates and appropriations. A brief overview of most of the agencies shows a huge discrepancy between what the agency is mandated to accomplish and what the taxpayers money is appropriated to accomplish and what is actually being done. Truman in his autobiography admits he did not properly study executive orders, and legislation he signed at the urging of people who told him it was Roosevelt's dying wish for the legislation to be signed, and he felt it was a mistake and had created secret government. Eisenhower, in his final speech to the nation warned the people that there were secret self interested persons taking over. It is time for the people to look back and see how we have given away some of our rights and how to reclaim them.

This does not mean ANOTHER agency, there are several agencies already in The Manual to oversee, but they do not seem to be doing their job. A prime example is the Department of Education. One of the missions stated for the Department of Education is to ENSURE an equal access to excellence in education anywhere Federal funds are being utilized. Yet we only have to go to any kindergarten to find that children in a public school in any wealthy area has a higher standard of education than those in impoverished areas. I completed an informal study while being paid to teach Youth Protection Act in many public school districts. I merely asked the students to recite the Pledge of Allegiance and we discussed what the words mean. Most of the students in impoverished areas did not even know that America is a country, not a county, nor did they know what

States were and many did not even know what State they lived in. This was during the week after 9/11/01. The other words of the Pledge were beyond them. These classes went to eighth grade. I taught at TWO prestigious pre schools and kindergartens, the children there ALL knew how many continents there are, what their names are, that they live in the United States, and they knew the fundamentals of space, math and science by January of their kindergarten as they are then being tested into prestigious private schools and HAVE to know this information.. NONE of these were taught at the public schools at that grade level.

As part of the Pomona Parent Project for high risk youth and their family, I was training high risk youth prior to their release to home secured life, they had ankle radio GPS equipment, and were in a special program. We trained the parents as well. This program costs the State or County $35 a family. NOT child, NOT per week, or day, only one state has taken the main Parent Project as its mandatory parenting program and guide and mandated ALL education staff at the public schools go through the programs, so their whole education program is on the same page. Since one of the major parts of the program is to include both the students and the parents in the programs as training volunteers, and then trainers, the program is outreaching, very sensitive to local school area, and culture as well as languages.

Instead, private juvenile facilities are springing up all over the country at an average cost to taxpayers of in some States $7,000 a month per youth. Where is Health and Human Services? Where is the oversight over our taxpayer dollars. I do not know about you, but I would surely rather spend a year or two on a tiered living program for a family that will turn out good citizens and taxpayers then to waste $7,000 a MONTH on facilities that at 18 turn monsters out on the public. It would be less expensive and more positive to put all these starving children in jail! At least in juvenile lock ups they would have been expected to keep their grades up, attend therapy and support programs, in the private foster care there have been a number of expose articles and televised magazine shows indicating the children are in expensive private education programs that upon investigation often did not even have a teacher, let alone a credentialed special education teacher.

Parenting, foster care, juvenile healthcare, proper exercise, education and juvenile rehabilitation are all parts of education, where is the Department of Education? Where is the Department of Health and Human Services? The Maslow Pyramid of solid person building mandates that a child have a solid base to build upon. How is having abandoning, or neglectful, or not adequate parents added to teachers, police, judges, caseworkers, counselors, jailers, foster care professionals, psychologists and the huge number of staff in all of these programs supposed to give a child that one person solid base necessary for building a solid personality? It will not, says Maslow.

Therefore, solid science, which most, if not all modern juvenile psychology is built upon is simply ignored in the bureaucracy of agencies mandated to care for, educate and rehabilitate our American juveniles for maximum possibility of building solid citizens who will not only have life, liberty and the ability to pursue happiness, but caring, empathetic citizens who will give back to others their best opportunity to have life, liberty and supported pursuit of happiness. There is not one word, in any of the enabling legislation used to appropriate taxpayer money for juvenile and family support that suggests Congress meant to create heartless, rule overridden, and unscientifically based programs that meet paperwork standards rather than support the best possible start for every juvenile in the United States of America.

As an example the State mandates for food for each child in lock downs makes no sense. One facility I researched had a wonderful chef, who had put in a salad and baked potato bar to facilitate better nutrition. The State regulations did not allow her to do that, it had to be put in the adult dining room, and youth had to ask for special permission to eat there AFTER they had eaten the prescribed meals on their units. A five year old was given the exact same plate as a fourteen year old during his/her growth years. The five year old was throwing out food, and had no interest in a salad bar to inspire to clean the plate, the fourteen year old was hungry and not getting proper nutrition. If their staff did not have enough staff to accompany fourteen year olds to the salad and baked potato bar, they simply had to go to bed hungry. BUT the paperwork showed all was well.

In closing: It is so obvious in creation of a synopsis of our Manual of the United States Government, that our leadership has been conscientious, not just of the compassion needed to help those in dire need, but also of the need to promote the programs that help, and let go of those, giving them feet to stand on, roots to grow with, and dreams to pass along to those who come after them. What had gone wrong? Each of those in every agency I surveyed had many ideas of how to make their own job, and agency more effective and less costly, but they said, over and over, they are always interviewing, surveying and asking for our thoughts, and then do just what they want to, ignoring our input completely. That is a sad statement if true.

In the first draft, I had intended to use the five papers I wrote for my PhD, which even with a 3.74 average, and five papers, did not get the APA approval, since I could not afford the $16,000 for an edit, I had been told it would be in my financial aid package. After working on the book at urging of friends for some time, I changed the format. I will not therefore include the actual papers or bibliography. I have utilized The Manual of the United States Government (2004, 2008) instead, with a synopsis of the agencies. Many of the agencies included the statement, they would be discussed in further depth later in the book, or in other agency review. I also decided that I would put in the parts involving other agency review, but except for the above, not go into further depth for this book on any agency. That was because, upon completion, I felt that the United States Government has had a large array of dreams, visions, and managed to bring them to fruition as far as being active agencies approved and established by Congress.

It is up to the people who pay for them to make sure they are still needed, and are doing the job paid to do.

Now we seem to need to choose one that interests each of us, and help the employees and often the leadership to get them freed to do what they were intended to do. I heard so many amazing ideas and met not one person in my interviews who did not want their agency to be more people and result oriented than paperwork dull. SO, I am going to leave it to Americans to choose and support a cause of your choice.

God Bless America.

There are so many people, with dreams and hard work at making this earth be what I believe the Creator of this earth meant it to be: An abundant short dance in the balance with nature. Science in all its wisdom has begun to realize that the smaller they are able to see science, the more connected they see it is. One Rabbi gave a talk about the existence of God or not, his opinion was, that an item as small as a toothpick, has an office filled with plans, for the workers, for the machines, for the types of wood used, and if a tiny item such as a toothpick needs such plans, how much more likely that something as complex as the universe has to have some kind of plan and planner. Not one ably identified or consulted by any human dancing here for this short life, but some entity, as many human belief systems have embraced, larger than any of us, and longer lasting than our tiny short run each on this earth

The Founders of the United States wrote "freedom OF Religion" for many reasons, to study those reasons is fascinating, and in part is used to end the centuries, and centuries of war humans justified as "religious" wars. The Founders did not all have the same religions, it was a great resolution on their part to come to the agreement that everyone had the RIGHT to their religion, but there would never be a STATE religion to avoid the conflicts other nations had over the centuries about whose side GOD was on..

Nelson Mandela, invented the concept of an entire segment of the globe having hearings and saying what they had suffered, what they had done, what they had been part of, and then to forgive and rebuild together. He implemented it with soccer games and public hearings. The read of those hearings is while horrifying and heartbreaking is so innovative and healing it is an important part of education for all persons on this earth.

Jesus, Mohammed, Buddha, Mother Teresa, Ghandi, all had the opportunity and background to be one of the rich, and find a niche for taking as much as they could, yet none of them did. Instead they used their education and compassion for people to attempt to lead people to a more peaceful and productive life for all.

These persons give us only a tiny view of what we can do to make this world a better place.

For everyone.

Recently I was watching a documentary about the no more war, and no more draft movements in America and then saw someone talking about Saul Alinsky. I had heard a lot of campaign rhetoric that those who studied with Alinsky, or used his methods were all communists and socialists. And I thought of the book by Dan Stockman, the financial advisor to Reagan who admitted the entire idea of trickle down economics had failed and just about destroyed America,

Each of us needs to know our rights, and what it is we are REALLY doing out in the world to "give" those rights to others.

Then we need to put those concepts together and make this world be what it can be, IF we want it to.......we can kill ourselves, or sigh, and wait for the next texting driver, or drunk, or insane person to shoot us at the local market or in our own living room so they can get money for drugs.

Or we can spread hate, and rant and protest, and go home and think we have made the world a better place. Then we can get on our computers and spread more hate and ignorance......OR, choose one thing out of our own self initiated list of concerns and begin to ask our elected officials what they are doing, and if they do not have time for them, vote them out. Run for office. Support someone who WILL listen to you and your city and get things resolved.

We can sigh and give up, and the greatest dream of human changing government OF the People, BY the PEOPLE, and FOR the PEOPLE will pass away, as all other big governance systems have in the past.

OR, we can BE Americans and fix the problems.........we are THE ONLY country that really gives US the responsibility. We can show others, not get enough military over there to force them to accept our ideals, how to build their own nations into real democracies to join United Nations and be one globe, all together in peace and abundance for ALL.

Thinking of Alinsky, I thought of all the good things he had done, helped workers get rights, and not be just energy for rich people (my Grandparents where factory owners, and land owners, and were VERY controlled by their political and religious beliefs to NOT be that kind of person) and he helped get people to realize education could help them.........and he helped people realize that we are NOT victims, we are Americans. That led to the following thoughts.

IF we are not part of the resolution, we are the problem. There are no innocent victims in a democracy, just the bad guys, and the children, old, and disabled and those who do nothing. Find a problem and resolve it. Find a need and fill it.

If you give a man a meal, you feed him, if you show a man how to fish, he can feed himself, if you show a human the way to build hatcheries, and to keep the water clean and pure, and the fish vibrant and with plenty of their food, and nature balanced and plentiful for the next seven generations, then you will begin to understand what Native persons around the globe are about.

Watching someone talk on CSPAN today, I wanted to say this: I DID get the opportunity
to see Saul and more importantly to know people who knew and loved him..........one of
the most important memories I have is of Joan Baez either talking about Saul, or she or
her mother writing about him. I am O L D and have lived a long life, not too great on the
details, BUT I today, at all times use what I think was his most important message. To
live free, and to live supporting humanitarian principles. The strange thing is.........being
the usual American mutt, of many races, cultures and religions.........I find that whether it
is the paraphrased Jewish motto of a friend of mine who lost much of his family in the
Concentration camps.....(if you are not nice enough to be nice, be smart enough to be
nice) or the more well known principles of Jesus (LOVE God and LOVE one another,
AS, we LOVE ourselves) or Native culture (Honor and respect our Creator, our Elders,
and LOVE the earth, the Elders, and all our Creator has given us from our first breath to
our last...........and leave the place better for the next seven generations, NOT grab it all
and leave a wasteland of destruction due to our greed...............that the message I best
loved from Saul was to LIVE free, and to respect and support the freedom of others, in
any humane way you can figure out.

Both Jerry Rubin and Abbie Hoffman used many of Saul's thoughts as they did what they
called "street theatre". not "against", but FOR in such a way that no one could miss it.
When they threw away money on wall street, and opened FREE stores all across the
nation, it was I felt, inspired by Joan and her Mom telling the chewing gum story of some
christian college where the students were not pleased with their restrictions. Alinsky is
alleged to have said, well, what CAN you do........they said chew gum, he asked, what do
you want to do? they said have dances and parties..........he said.......well, put gum on
everything and say, we will stop with the gum, when you give us the dances and parties
choice...........I loved it........Have no idea if it worked or not...........but when I was
working with gangs I went on down to two of the most deadly ghettoes in California, and
tapped on the windows of cars and asked the gangsters if this was in fact their territory,
and of course they said yes, then I took them on field trips to Balboa, Laguna and Beverly
Hills and pointed out the living conditions were often MORE crowded and the
apartments just as crummy, but LOOK at the difference, NO old cars, No gum on the

sidewalk, NO dirty yards, etc, etc, and certainly NO violence in the streets, the parks lush and everyone enjoying them not murders a minute as in those areas they came from. I said do you think Cheney lives like your 'hood......

I said, if code enforcement says clean it up, or fix the apartments, NOPE, but if YOU say clean it up and fix it up, those landlords will be out in the night doing it themselves............I asked them to WRITE to big stores, and businesses and ASK them what it would take for them to bring stores into their neighborhoods. They were surprised to find the answer was to clean it up, and reduce crime. .it did not exactly get to that point, but the people in those areas cleaned up and helped each other..........and it all came back to stories about chewing gum and dances alleged to have originated with Saul Alinsky.............people need to know, we are AMERICANS, not old country serfs asking for our meanest of rights, we are not sweat shop slaves asking pathetically for ten minutes to go potty, and a restroom to go in the building..........we are AMERICANS.........and it is time to stop FIGHTING the government and to stop playing good cop.bad cop with two parties that BOTH just want the power and our taxpayer money.......who let THAT get passed, it is unConstitutional..........and unAmerican..........and we have laws to protect us, but BOTH parties have let them slip away so someONE whoever it is, can WIN, they just don't get it.........by ruining our vision........instead of building it and expanding it.......the great THEY have just about put us BACK to serfdom and slavery........but, we have the Constitution and we CAN still chew gum.

God bless America. And God forgive the humans.

Additional information:

This information is included as it was created as part of the work for a Doctoral paper and research on Health and Human Services and Human Health Programs. The way in which health CARE programs are evaluated was being explored and researched as indicated in the pages of the book regarding Health and Human Services. Each of the projects invented, researched and either implemented, or given to other groups to implement is a part of a vision of Reassessing and Restructuring Public Agencies for oversight and incentives to make each agency renew and restructure itself to keep doing what is needed until that need is filled and the agency can close its doors with honor and success.

Tia Maria Torres, the Director of the Villalobos Pitbull Rescue says on each of her shows, that she is living her passion, in hope of one day not needing to do it anymore. That heartfelt statement made me think that is what every public agency, or private charity needs to have as their mission.......to be impassioned to help those who need help, and to work hard to be put out of a job.

The following are projects we have designed.

Spirit Horse II Manual Spirit Horse II-Certification of Animals and Humans in program

Spirit Horse II warns everyone: Do NOT rely on movies and television shows about horses. Horses are huge wild animals. One bee sting, or bad injury or illness can turn the sweetest horse into a dangerous half ton of danger for humans. DO NOT ever forget that a horse is a horse, not a human or a pet. Learn the horse safety rules and obey them for the safety of everyone and the animals. Those feet are covered in either aluminum or steel, have respect for them. Do NOT ever walk behind horses, let horses know you are approaching, do NOT startle them. They kick when defending themselves.

Animals certified in Spirit Horse II are trained using the Delta Animal Certification videos and training manuals. The animals for Delta Certification are going to be working with severely disabled or hospitalized children and adults. The animals working in Spirit Horse II are working with active, and often high risk clients. The need for our own certification process led us to develop our own criteria, for certification, but Delta is a wonderful and humane system for training therapy animals, or pets, we encourage anyone to use their website to purchase and complete their online or in person courses.

Spirit Horse II is also dedicated to the ideal that all of our animals are our partners in a business created to help heal others. Whether human or animal. Therefore, once an animal is accepted into Spirit Horse II, it cannot be sold and must be provided care for life. Spirit Horse II does not ask our volunteers to stop volunteering as they age or become disabled. An ear, an audience for class, extra eyes to watch everyone for safety are always welcome.

The major difference between certifications for Delta and Spirit Horse II is the need for Delta animals to be quieter, and score higher on skills assessment certification testing. A Spirit Horse animal may be old, disabled, or not able to perform regulatory testing to the standard of Delta, but still is well able to perform safely and in good health for Spirit Horse II members.

For example: A young, bouncy dog that is not able to pass the rigorous sit and stay tests for Delta Certification may be just what Spirit Horse II needs for young students who are very well able to deal safely with a dog bouncing and jumping around them. In a Delta program, the same dog would be unsafe for a hospitalized patient.

Another example is the need for many equine therapy programs to have mid age range horses with no stumbling in their gait. In Spirit Horse II, there are few programs that exist in our work that do not find a stumbley horse to be an advantage for several reasons. We therefore often accept therapeutic horses from other programs when they begin to falter, or are felt to be too unsteady for their programs. We have a 39 year old Arabian quarter mile racing horse that was out to stud for 12 years before he was sold down. We rescued him and he is one of our most in demand horses. He no longer is expected to have riders, but he is a trainer for wrapping legs, putting on performance or health care boots, and other stall or performance care projects. He loves the attention, the students love that he is extremely safe for them. Most of our students, by the time they reach higher levels of performance grooming are deeply in love with this horse, and really glad of a chance to learn show standard braiding with him, rather than on a young show horse.

Our certifications are made by our Directing Trainer, our veterinarian, our physical therapists, and psychologists together. Each animal has a file that lists his or her latest certification review. The tag for each animal contains a notation of exactly what areas that animal is certified for. We also use animals that are in process of gaining a level of competence and experience to be certified, their tags are noted as "in training". Many of our animals are owned by trainers, staff, volunteers and community members. None of our animals is ever sold down. In the event that the vet recommends euthanasia, our animals are humanely put down. We feel death is part of life, and the responsible care of animals includes the reality that in captivity animals often outlive their own health. We feel this is an educational part of our program, as well as part of our responsibility model in animal care and training.

Levels of competency are:

1. Behavior. Our team assesses our animals prior to accepting them into the program and periodically during the year, or if an incident or concern is raised by a rider, staff, volunteer, or therapists. We expect our animals to behave in a safe and non-aggressive manner towards humans and other animals. Our human therapists and assistants are all required to be certified in our own program levels as described in our certification material.
2. Health. Our team and our vet assesses our animals twice a year. Each animal is assessed each day by staff and therapists. The Directing Trainer may be asked to make a decision about soundness for the day's activities. The vet techs and vet are the final opinion as to whether an animal is fit for the day's activity. Any animal not sound will be referred to the vet for care until released back to work. All humans must have an annual check up from their personal physician for doing the level of work they are doing in Spirit Horse II programs.
3. Training. Our animals are utilized for a variety of programs. Each animal has a file that contains the areas that animal is certified for or is in training for. All animals are rigorously trained to accept wheelchairs, canes, crutches, and personal hygiene products attached to the riders. Animals in training may have issues, this is covered in our orientation with our riders and staff. We feel it is important for our riders to be aware that while our goal is to educate animal owners to have their animals safe around disabled persons, it is not reality, and the disabled persons need to be aware of animals that are not as well trained as ours and be safe. Therefore, we train our animals on site and with real riders, not just with our own staff using similar healthcare equipment and items.
4. Care. Our animals are expected to be cared for by many classes and private riders each day. Our staff uses files and office day boards to make sure each animal is bathed regularly, is fed appropriately and has seen the shoer and other animal care experts as necessary. A big part of our program is to have the participants take care of the animals, therefore most animals are cared for in a daily routine several times each day. Each animal has its own living area as the Directing Trainer and vet certify. Our animals are not loaned or rented out.

5. Safety. Both animals and humans are expected to use safety gear as suggested by the activity. Adults "may" sign a waiver and refuse to wear safety riding helmets only for exhibitions. At all other times even adult riders must wear regulation safety helmets. All riders are given an orientation in horse, and other animal safety and will be written up and may be excused from the program if they fail to follow safety regulations. ALL staff and volunteers are trained to address safety issues, and if necessary to contact the day Director, or the Spirit Horse II Director to handle issues. Safety stirrups are of choice. All performance level riders are to use the standard for the sport. Which often does not include safety stirrups. ALL staff are to realize that the ONLY riders to utilize safety belts, are those who work in a small round corral, with at least four horse handlers, a physical therapist and a specifically seat belt safety trained horse. Spirit Horse II considers being attached in any way to a horse to be inherently life threatening and is not to be done except as described above for severely physically disabled riders. The use of a safety belt is only with the presence of the physical therapist, and upon written prescription of the attending physician to the rider. The use of a safety belt is only with the written permission of both parents, or legal guardians.

6. The safety rules are to be posted and in at least two languages at all sites. ALL riders with different language needs are to be given the safety orientation in their own language, and to sign waivers in their own language. Spirit Horse II prefers that all riding members learn commands, and horse safety cues in English. In an emergency, the person needing to be heard may not know any other language. When riding on trails, in shows, and in rental stables, the only language may be English. Spirit Horse II feels it is important to know all safety cues in English.

7. There is NO horseplay allowed. While we encourage fun, and to experience joy with animals and while riding, no horseplay is allowed. The Spirit Horse II philosophy is that these ALL are wild animals. No matter how reliable, an animal, or even a human can reach a breaking point. It is extremely important to have all participants, whether staff, volunteers, riders or guests to be in compliance. They will get one warning, then be asked to leave the premises. This includes, but it not limited to unsafe horse activities, bullying, name calling, gossip, cliques, and practical jokes. We consider all of these negative behaviors.

8. NO smoking around horses, riders, guests or barns. When the stable and barns are closed, the staff and volunteers "may" designate one safe smoking area, however, Spirit Horse II is a non-smoking environment during work hours and in the stables and hay barns. Riders need to respect that the stables and barns are used for literacy and high risk youth programs. No smoking is part of the health education program for all of our programs and needs to be respected.
9. Recycling and no littering are both taught and upheld. Part of the Spirit Horse II program is to teach respect for the earth and the personal responsibility of each human to take part in not polluting, and not littering our earth, oceans, and other environmental resources.
10. NO FOOD is allowed to be brought on the site. Snacks, and meals are served as part of the nutrition programs, many foods are deadly to the animals and must be kept out of our environment. Carrots, apples, mints, and other horse snacks, approved dog and other small animal treats are available from staff. NO ANIMALS are to be fed without asking a staff person. Horses and dogs often eat food wrappers. This can be deadly. The small cellophane straw wrappers from juice boxes are often eaten, and become glued to the intestines of horses. Dogs and other therapy animals. They cause serious infections and death. DO NOT bring any food or drinks to the sites.
11. Shots. Our animals and handlers are all vaccinated regularly. Tetanus is the most common vaccine needed by visitors to stables. Staph infections, in the cleanest of stables is a constant threat WASH YOUR HANDS. Food staff wears gloves for preparation and serving of food. Stables that have reptiles have a threat of salmonella as well. WASH YOUR HANDS after any contact with the reptiles, ducks, or chickens.
12. ILLNESS. Please do NOT come to Spirit Horse II ill. Many of our riders are disabled and their health compromised. They do not need your cold, sore throat, or flu. If you have taken antibiotics for 48 hours, and your doctor feels you may safely return to the program, you may, but are not required to take class, work or volunteer when ill. Our riders health is too important to compromise. Horses also are very subject to illness. Do not bring outside horses, tack or items to our stable areas without permission and proper disinfecting procedures being taken. WASH YOUR HANDS when you arrive to make sure you do not spread something from your own pets to our working partners.

EXTENDED PROGRAMS

Spirit Horse II has many ongoing expanded programs which include high risk Boy Scouts of America Venture Crew programs, juvenile probation and regional center vendors who bring their clients to the programs. The programs for children of veterans, and active duty service personnel, as well as children of first responders are included in the veteran's service project.

Many of our programs include performance and exhibition teams and private riding programs for riders who have advanced beyond treatment programs.

Our staff and volunteers enjoy the use of many of our program facilities at all times as long as they do not interfere with ongoing treatment classes. Spirit Horse II gives a series of exhibition programs in partnership with local parks and schools to give the opportunity of our programs to children, teens and adults who may never have any other chance to experience a real working horse environment. We trailer horses to events in partnership with juvenile probation, parks, and local police and sheriff events. We have our own Spirit Horse II safety regulations for this type of event. ALL staff and volunteers have to complete a special training program and be certified before being allowed to attend a trailered out event.

Spirit Horse II encourages our riders, staff and volunteers to do exhibit and performance riding in shows, parades, and other events. Each of these events must be approved by the Training Director in writing prior to being announced publicly, if the name National Homes for Heroes/Spirit Horse II is used to promote the event.

Spirit Horse II encourages media coverage and filming. Each of our riders is notified and signs a waiver that encompasses the most open relationship with media and the entertainment industry. Any problems are to be reported immediately to the Training Director in writing.

INCIDENT REPORTING-Youth Protection Act

Spirit Horse II utilizes a system of Government Mandated and Trained Youth Protection and protection of the disabled that is supported by our systems rules.

NUMBER ONE: BUDDY system. When a person signs in to Spirit Horse II, they must be signed in with a buddy. At no time are the two buddies to lose sight of each other!

NUMBER TWO: Log book. If there is a complaint or incident, it MUST be reported in writing to the stable day staff in writing in the log book. Orientation includes the warning that if an incident is not reported within 24 hours and the appropriate incident report filed, it did not happen! There are no exceptions.

We train ALL of our membership that when someone says "don't tell", you have to "tell". If no one else, speak directly to the Training Director.

NUMBER THREE: The incident report includes all relevant information. Each site director is responsible within 48 hours of a log in to put the incident in the computerized log book for Spirit Horse II and to submit a copy of the incident report electronically. Hard copy is to be kept on site for ONE YEAR. All hard copy is sent after one year to the Training Director, then to the lawyers for safe keeping for twenty-five (25) years.

If any person, complainant, staff or Training Director feels the complaint involves child abuse, it must be reported to the police within one hour of notification of the log keeper. The "Buddy" statement is required on the incident report and must be taken immediately. ALL other witnesses or potential witness must be identified on the incident report. When parents are calling to report an incident they are expected to go over the entire incident report with the complainant and the Buddy prior to filing. Mandatory mediation and /or dispute resolution are to be instituted immediately upon request by the Training Director. ALL records must be kept for one year with the incident report, and filed electronically with Spirit Horse II as they are filed on site.

The Training Director will have all of these files kept in hard copy for twenty-five years, by a Law Firm on retainer for this purpose only.

Horses, animals and youth are a prescription for injuries. Spirit Horse II has a prescribed regulatory method to deal with injuries.

1. CALL 911 IF NECESSARY THEN, CALL THE PARENTS if they are not present. FIND THE TRAINING DIRECTOR.

2.Fill in the log, fill out the incident report. Take pictures if possible. GET
THE BUDDY STATEMENT.

3. ALL adults are also required to be within sight of another certified adult
at all times. ANY problems may be put in the log and handled by the
Training Director or the site Director and referenced to the Training
Director.

4.ALL adults are required to have live scan fingerprints done periodically
for staff, or volunteers at any Spirit Horse II site. Parents are encouraged to
accompany their children to all classes and events. Grandparents, paid
parenting staff are encouraged to accompany children. ALL visitors and
rider family members MUST be logged in and given a day-pass that limits
areas they are to be allowed. Parents, Grandparents, and other guests are to
stay within eyesight of the rider they are visiting. This is to make sure no
one's guests are wandering around treatment and youth areas without staff
supervision.

For safety: Spirit Horse II utilizes one type of handicapped accessible
restroom for riders and guests. Staff and volunteers have their own
restrooms. ONE person in the restroom at a time, ONE buddy waiting
outside for safety. ADULTS are requested not to linger near the restrooms,
and to be accompanied by their assigned staff or buddy for their own safety
as well as that of the riders. False abuse claims are damaging to adults: Spirit
Horse II asks all adults to adhere to the rules to minimize risk to our
juveniles, and disabled persons, and to minimize risk of false claims against
adults.

Some types of emergency:

LOOSE HORSE.

A loose horse in a highly populated stable area is very dangerous. Even a
usually calm horse may get frightened and trample someone if too many
people try to catch the horse, or are just in the way.

If you hear someone yell "loose horse" move close to a building, or tree, or
vehicle. Stand still, and if the horse approaches, wave your arms to wave the
animal away. Do NOT yell, or scare the horse further. Let horse staff

retrieve the animal ONLY. If you, or someone near you is in a wheelchair, or on crutches, get as close as possible to a very large object, tree, vehicle, or inside until the horse is caught. Please help wheelchair and other persons who need help. Safety is the utmost importance.

FALLEN RIDER

When a rider falls, stand still. If you are on horseback, stop the horse and stand still. Let the staff take care of the emergency. If you are asked to dismount and return your animal to the barn early, do it. The safety of the person who has fallen is more important than if your class was cut short.

LISTEN TO THE STAFF. The staff will direct everyone safely. Please listen and do as you are asked.

Do NOT chase the rider's horse. Let staff take care of recapturing the horse and calming the situation down.

IN THE ARENA OR ROUND CORRAL

DO NOT tie horses to the fences. EVER.

LOOK to see if another horse is in the arena, or round corral before opening the gate.

Follow directions of staff around the horses when working in the arena and/or round corrals.

WASHING HORSES

Spirit Horse II has allowed two philosophies. The first is to NEVER tie a horse while grooming and washing. Either a second person holds the horse, or the rider is certified to handle a horse alone and takes care of both holding the horse and washing it or grooming it. Many of our horses are groomed prior to riding in their own stalls and are NOT tied up. Follow the directions of staff.

The second philosophy is people who believe in cross tying. Follow the directions and learn safety around cross tied horses. While Spirit Horse II does not believe in this practice, many of our horses are privately owned. Their owners have used cross tying and are not comfortable with natural horsemanship grooming techniques. Therefore, we allow this exception to our rule.

SHOERS

When the shoers are working, EVERONE is to pay attention to the requests of the shoer. Some horses are very stressed by shoeing and need quiet and to be left alone. Other horses like a human handler to hold them, others are tied to a post and fine. Listen to the shoers. They are hired for their expertise and know when a horse is not feeling well and behaving poorly. It is not up to riders or guests to say "but I know this horse, he loves me". Listen and be safe, the shoers need to be safe, and the horses need to be safe.

VETS

When the vets are tending horses, everyone must listen to the vet and vet techs and do as they ask. These are professionals who need to be safe around huge, injured or ill animals. Spirit Horse II wants riders, guests and volunteers to experience all aspects of horse care, however, when the vet or vet tech asks for people to leave the scene. Do so at once. Quietly.

OTHER ANIMALS in the programs.

Many volunteers and staff bring their own dogs and other pets to share with the riders and their families. The animals are in training, or certified animal assisted therapy course completion animals. PLEASE treat all animals with respect and care. It can be overwhelming for an animal to be rushed by several persons. Think about how you would feel, and be respectful of the animals. Mother animals are often vicious in protecting their young. ASK before handling any baby animals, chickens, ducks, or going near mares with foals.

Mares who are about to foal often are guided by their instinct to be alone, they may bite or kick, when usually they are gentle and safe horses. Do not bother the mares, ASK staff for permission before approaching them.

FOAL imprinting and colt development

Spirit Horse II is a NativeAmericanNaturalHorsemanship practicing program. We believe that horses do not need to be hit, kicked, or abused into obeying. We also have trainers who have trained with vets and trainers who practice foal imprinting and colt development. In the first hours of a young horse's life the trainers and vet techs will work with the animal to imprint many later working skill lessons on the young horse. In colt development, similar exercises are done to prepare the young horse for a seamless and easy transition to a rideable horse. Please do not interfere in these sessions.

Spirit Horse II-therapuetic modality descriptions

Equine Assisted Literacy Program

Spirit Horse II has credentialed special education teachers who have created their own literacy programs that include, but are not limited to reading, writing and learning about horses. The programs are designed with the IEP or approval of the treating doctor (if any) to facilitate a joy of learning and increase age and grade level skills.

Public school programs that promote reading are part of our free community projects that each Spirit Horse II site will participate in locally, and Spirit Horse II will participate in nationally and internationally to promote literacy.

Freeworldu.org is utilized by Spirit Horse II as a free mentoring program.

Family literacy programs are Spirit Horse II programs that encourage families to learn old family stories, to find out facts and history of the family and to share these stories in our international literacy project.

Physical Therapy-Equine assisted physical therapy programs are in two programs.

The Equine assisted therapy program is accomplished with the prescription of a doctor or psychologist. Many of the students in this program are accompanied by their county approved vendors from regional treatment centers. The staff is expected to accompany and stay with the riders at all times and to fill out the one sheet observation page to be returned to the prescribing doctor. Spirit Horse II does not keep any records, it is the responsibility of the staff and prescribing physician.

The Equine Therapy program also requires a prescribing physician or psychiatrist, if necessary. Spirit Horse II has licensed and certified equine therapists who work at the sites. Spirit Horse II Equine Therapists fill out a one page, numbered observation sheet for each class and mail it to the prescribing physician or psychiatrist. THESE records are kept electronically for ONE WEEK only in case of loss in the mail.

Emotional Equine Assisted Therapy

Programs for high risk youth and children of vets and active duty service personnel, as well as Mommy and Me Ride, and Daddy and Me Ride programs are non –specific and have staff that is certified to work in our own unique Spirit Horse II programs. These all were developed and are overseen by our own psychologists and behavioral specialists.

These programs are offered free to community projects such as Juvenile Probation, Housing, schools, Head Start, religious and Scouting programs.

These programs include: Kids Anonymous (a program for teens in divorce, death or other stressful situations) and Kids Jr (a program for children in divorce, death or other stressful situations), 12 Steps Home (for vets and their families) and 12 Steps Home from Betrayal by Brothers at Arms (for vets who have been sexually assaulted in combat zones). These are quasi twelve step programs developed by the kids, and the vets themselves. Spirit Horse II is in the process of finding out how, or if, they can become real 12 step programs. As in all 12 step programs peer support, rather than professionals is the rule. While adult supervisors or staff are present for the children and teen programs, they are there for safety, not to interfere in the process. We called AA and asked how to become real 12 Step programs, they said to email the programs. We did. We have never heard yay or nay, so still are considering ourselves quasi-12 Step.

Meditation, yoga, stress reduction, anger management, mediation programs

Programs to help our staff, riders, families and guests improve their lives are offered on a continuous basis. Most of these programs are free of charge and open to the public if the space is available.

Spirit Horse II refers all drug, alcohol and other addicts to outside programs and treatment.

Gardening and Green programs

Plants, animals and the outdoors are a part of the therapeutic environment at Spirit Horse. Grooming, care of tack and stables and kennels and other animal areas is part of the program. Spirit Horse II does not allow anyone to come to a program without full participation in all areas of animal care, and group programs where required by Spirit Horse II.

Art, Drama, Music programs

Art in many forms, Drama, Music and Dance are all a part of programs offered at Spirit Horse II.

Field Trips and family inclusive events

From work done with the Y WINGS programs in the wake of Desert Storm, Spirit Horse II started a program of field trips and family inclusive events, such as trips to rodeos, horse shows, parades, and performances or school programs for other members to show support. Spirit Horse II has a credentialed teacher to schedule field trips. Fundraising is utilized to help reduce the cost and scholarships to families as needed are a goal of each event or field trip. We use school bus service local to each Spirit Horse II site for transportation. Children who do not have a family adult to accompany them are encouraged to be included as part of another family approved by their parents or guardians. Spirit Horse II is a diversity supporting program and refrains from calling a family a "mom and dad and kids". Many children in high risk programs have parents in service, or prison, or dead. Spirit Horse II uses our education programs and events to help children include others, rather than exclude or identify "otherness" as a negative for children already deeply stressed by their realities.

Spirit Horse II has specific events for children of terminally ill parents or siblings. These were created by AIDS Project Pasadena many years ago, and Spirit Horse II feels this type of event gives a day of support to hurting children. Each child is paired with two pre-approved adult family members, friends, or staff and volunteers to have a complete day, even in a group, just for them.

Spirit Horse II has an open door ride free policy for terminally ill patients and their families to come and observe and participate as much as possible in any of our classes and events.

From Cowboy life-skill classes to stressed executives who volunteer and feed carrots and groom horses a few hours a month, Spirit Horse II shares a moment of respite from a world that is outside the gates. As our vet told us "when a horse comes here, they have it made", we hope this is true for our staff, riders, and volunteers and guests at all times. We strive for that to be our service.

FORMS-SPIRIT HORSE II

HORSE REGISTRATION FORM

Name of horse:
Nickname (if one):
Date horse came to Spirit Horse:
Stall number:
Owned by:
Address and phone number for owner:
Preferred vet: or signature of owner to use our own
vets_____date_____
Age of horse
Mare/Colt/Stallion/Gelding
History of horse

Last known shots, worming, known medical needs, special feed needs, special shoeing needs

Please attach horse worming and vaccination table and put horse on next stable schedule for worming and vaccinations.

BE specific, what will owner be doing with horse, and what days will owner want to use horse so it will be unavailable for class work. Remind owners to let us know in advance of special events, or performances when horse will be out of Spirit Horse II.

Date	Vaccinations	Worming	Shoer	Bathed (list whole month in column)

THE TURTLE MEDICINE LODGE PROJECT

The Turtle Medicine Lodge Project was named Turtle Lodge in honor of the dream of Manitoba Elder David Courchene, Anishnabe Nation, Eagle Clan. After a lifetime dream, he built the first Turtle Lodge in Manitoba to carry the message of hope and peace. The Turtle Medicine Lodges will carry this message to many Native Nations and utilize the knowledge that Elder David Courchene teaches in classes, conferences First Nations events to share a knowledge he believes can act as the founation in supporting New Life in Mother Earth is now entering and that the Elders have confirmed has arrived. The Turtle Medicine Lodges will encourage all persons of all nations to contact turtlelodge.org for more information.

Each of the Native American nations, both the 567 recognized sovereign nations, and those urban and mixed culture Native Nations members as well as Native Nations across the world (we found there are still existing Native Nations survivors of the british tribe and many other european countries)are encouraged to use the plans for Turtle Medicine Lodges to explore and rekindle ancient culture, language and belief and help all humans restore balance to nature and life.

The physical designs for the project included 20 too thousand acre sites as retreats, and healing spaces, as educational, and ceremonial places to encompass the local traditions as well as science and technology and newly invented things to keep our world a pleasant and wonderful place to live and share these ancient philosophies.

Two of the goals of Turtle Medicine Lodge were to help groups of Native people get together and work together to salvage their past, to grow beyond the horrifying genocide they have survived, and to grow in a positive way not just remain stuck in a past that no longer exists. To use science and technology to renew, and rekindle the balance of nature.

This section is the proposal summary for what we call the "48 Acres" or three tiered human development sites.

Three Tiered Treatment and Housing Systems

"48 Acres"

The drawing is for 48 acres or more. The scale is left out to show the idea, rather than the exact site. Each site, of course, due to local code enforcment, permits, building codes, etc and location, will have to be unique and done exactly when the land is acquired. Each site will be created for its exact purpose. These purposes have included Domestic Violence Survivors programs, Senior housing, Disabled housing, Independent Mental Illness treatment and independent living projects, veteran and veteran family programs, refugee relocation and city redevelopment programs.

BEFORE land is acquired inquiries need to be made to get the support of the local city council and preliminary thoughts from the building and zoning departments as to how hard it will be to create reality on that exact piece of land before beginning to estimate costs and break the project down into doable units. IF you have military base, VA or HUD property it is much easier to deal with, as the agencies deal with the land acquirement and use politics.

The 48 acre and more sites will ALL have level one and two apartments, townhouses and condos. In each area the local developers will be contacted for support on tier three new housing, especially for veterans needing physical disability modifications in the housing prior to the designs being submitted to building and zoning. If redeveloping an area, both investors and developers

Private parking will be available for all units, handicapped parking will be designated throughout the acreage as well. Near the arenas, physical therapy, water therapy and gardens as well as the equine therapy barns and/or round corrals will be parking for busses and vans as necessary. Vans and busses will be scheduled as much as possible on pick up/drop off of one group after another to minimize the number of empty vehicles parked at any one time. The sites will have shuttle service on the lap road. Disabled person transport will be available as well. The goal is to have flex solar energy systems on all parking structures and roofed areas to accomplish with wind resources a negative power use for the complexes. Several research projects and private companies have been approached on this goal and say it is possible and easily accomplished. Some major electric suppliers, including municipal and private energy companies have been approached and say this is easily accomplished, and they are already approved for training and working with veterans. It is suggested that first time offenders in low income areas by given the opportunity to train and hired for this type of job in restructuring rural and urban low cost housing areas. Both Probation and Parole have been approached on this approach to innovative probation and parole programs and have said, yes, let us know as it begins. The Veteran Courts, and Veteran Legal programs have all said YES to this as a proposed rehabilitation and career training program for which they are already funded.

The forty eight and larger acreage sites will have recruited training facilities from chain stores and restaurants to serve the tenants on the site, to serve outside patrons during regular store hours, and to train veterans for jobs when they leave the tier one and tier two living sites. NHH/SH2 is active in recruiting service companies and installation companies for disabled housing as appropriate for large nearby developments and cities with veteran disabled populations that will create work installing and maintaining special equipment in third tier housing.

The gardens are the Horticultural Therapy portion of each of the sites. Flowers, fruits, vegetables are all included in the therapeutic gardens. The sites with apartments and townhouses ALL have small growing areas, the residents are expected to grow something, even if just lawn, or potted plants that they can use for their therapeutic time at home.

Some of the major fencing surrounding the pools, gardens, arenas, and outer security walls and fencing will have fruits, honeysuckle, vegetables, grapes and flowers growing so the residents and therapy members can feel free to help keep them up, and to eat the fruits, vegetables, berries and grapes.

Every site will have gray water retrieval to service the garden areas. The City of Pasadena has piloted and is modeling programs for this type of water retrieval. Cal Tech, among other Technology programs now have students doing research on using retrieved water from storms in many ways, both to reduce damage to the streets and sewers from major influx of storm water, and to increase available water resources in many areas. The Chairs of these programs have expressed interest in any site being used as a class project for their current students to design, build and implement the use of research programs, for which they are expected to raise their own funding as part of their degree requirements.

All of the sites will have as much solar as possible. We expect to show case the newest forms of solar water heating and other energy concepts by asking the companies to showcase their products and give discounts for any of the third tier homes that can afford them. Wind energy is also being researched, the fans are becoming smaller and much more effective at saving energy and transmitting it to local energy companies for use and storage. In all areas where a site is created wind energy use will be researched as well to reduce the costs to the residents, and give as many residents as possible an opportunity for jobs in these newly developing fields. Veterans we have found, are often funded for this type of work program through special veteran programs.

Green energy is part of the architecture, and it is part of the therapy. As the level two goal is to facilitate jobs for veterans and their family members, green energy is a growing field and veterans are encouraged to go to school to be cutting edge developers, and installers and maintainers of green energy sources for urban, suburban and rural areas. (when these sites are used for disabled, or senior, or low income residence three tier and first time home owner programs the on site job work, and inspiration for an education to work part time on their own site will be an additional positive goal for green programs.

The forty eight acre and bigger sites will be recruiting private dental programs (or Native American dental programs for Native American veteran based sites) and recruiting veterans and their family members to maintain long hour dental clinics in storefronts on the site to be rented out for that purpose. In areas where the VA will provide the dentists and equipment, the site will provide the dental clinic space and/or mobile dental clinics for the members of the site project.

10 and less acreage sites concept drawing:

This drawing is a concept for 10 or less acres. Even a one acre site can contain ONE level two house for the site supervising couple (at least one must be a vet, or active duty military) to live on the site.

The therapy buildings and modules will be added as the local zoning and building permits allow, and the land supports.

The ideal goal is to have local VA facilities send day program persons out to the sites in vans and by bus. These will go back and pick up other day members, and shuttle back and forth to the VA and base facilities to decrease parking needs, and annoyance to the local community from too much traffic.

Because veterans and active duty families are working, and in school, the programs are expected to start early in the day and extend late into the night, in order to promote maximum use of the program buildings and assets.

The ideal is for the VA to provide therapeutic support if we provide the rooms for therapy, the gyms for physical therapy, and the pools, and other therapeutic areas. This will allow Healthwalk to provide therapists and oversee the VA staff needs, and NHH/SH2 to only have to deal with independent living quarters. (Townhouses and condo's on site-and facilitating home ownership, or long term lease of homes off site for tier three). Which reduces the need for additional permits, state licensing, etc.

EDUCATION PROGRAMS: Many of the veteran and high risk program initiated and implemented education programs.

RACIAL AND BULLYING ABATEMENT PROGRAM

School programs to address the bullying of active duty and veteran children. As horrible as it seems, children often bully the children of active duty and veteran children. The parents are trained to go and talk to the schools, we also provide speakers as needed from local VFW or other veteran groups to assist the school in educating their students to stop this practice. Often it has been teachers and parents that have initiated the bullying.

One parent called us and told us the TEACHER had told her ten year old that she was lying, in front of the other students, that in fact her father was NOT in the military, and was NOT going to give her the present she told the other children she was going to get. The Social Worker from the local vet center had called our equine therapy program and told us one of her veterans, a thirteen year Marine who had lost his home and farm to a development fraud and job scam was overwhelmingly depressed that he could not keep his promise to his daughter to give her a horse for her eleventh birthday. I said send them on out, It was just a fluke that the day the little girl came out, we had had a surprise filly born from one of our rescued barrel racing horses. What a great heart warmer for that little girl to be told, your Dad has had some bad things happen to him, but he was so worried that he could not keep his promise to you, YOU can have our 23 horses, and little tiny filly for your own joy.

We also had just gotten three new therapy pups for training, as our four old therapy dogs were about ready to retire, and too large for me to take on the bus after being hit by drunks racing and being on crutches and braces. Friends would often give me rides, but they did not want big dogs in their cars.

I will never forget the joy of that little girl as she romped with those dogs, and another therapy dog that the foundation Director had brought that day. Who could not be heartwarmed as she was rolling on the floor playing with them, and screamed out, this is the best day of my life!

When I went with the Mother of the child, and told this story to that teacher, she was very saddened by her behavior. She agreed to help educate other teachers to watch out for and end bullying of children of veterans and active duty military. Most people are not mean, they are just ignorant, and when lovingly helped to understand, are great help in ending the horrors our children go through.

SPECIAL ACKNOWLEDGEMENTS

There are so many people who inspired me along the way. But of course my sons, Tim and Dean, my parents, and their ancestors on both sides for making me learn and love both sides of many an issue, My siblings, Homer, Deborah, Diana, Lisa, James, John, My sister Eva and sister (in law) Judy who passed away way too young. and all of my nieces, nephews, Grand nieces and Grand –nephews. My cousins. My God children and my extended family.......and friends.

My Native Nation and all those around the globe standing up for Native Nations and their right to exist as something other than slaves, dishwashers, or maids to those who take over their lands.

I want to thank President George W. Bush as I wrote to him when I started the academic experience of a Phd in Reassessing and Restructuring Public Agencies. I want to thank his then Chief of Staff of the White House Andrew Card, to whom my letter was passed, who encouraged me, and said, when you get this study completed, we need it, and gave me referrals to the agencies I was studying.

Most of all I want to thank the American people I worked with, and the agency personnel, from Secretaries, to Administrators, to day staff workers who helped me understand what COULD be from the legislated programs.

And I thank GOD.

We may not agree on what that entity is, or how to show respect and honor to God, but we are fortunate to live in a country where we have freedom to worship as we please, as long as our "worship" does not include harming others. And we respect those who do not believe in that entity, it is their legal right under the Constitution. What a great concept.

Turtle Medicine Lodge

Tag line goes here.

Tel:

Turtle Medicine Lodge

Turtle Medicine Lodges are based on the dream of Manitoba Elder David Courchene, Anishnabe Nation, Eagle Clan. After a lifetime dream, he built the first Turtle Lodge in Manitoba to carry a message of hope and peace.

The Turtle Medicine Lodges will carry this message to many Native Nations, and utilize the knowledge that David Courchene teaches in classes, conferences and First Nations events to share a knowledge he believes can act as the foundation in supporting the New Life that Mother Earth is now entering, and that the Elders have confirmed has arrived.

The Turtle Medicine Lodges will encourage all persons of all nations to contact turtlelodge.org for more information.

Cornish Designs

Cornish Designs

Phone:
Fax:
Email:

Back Panel Heading

This is a good place to briefly, but effectively, summarize your products or services. Sales copy is typically not included here.

Lorem ipsum dolor sit amet, consectetuer adipiscing elit, sed diem nonummy nibh euismod tincidunt ut lacreet dolor et accumsan.